Meditations of A Happy Homemaker

NOT A DESPERATE HOUSEWIFE

Mary Boyd Alley

Winters Publishing
P.O. Box 501
Greensburg, IN 47240

800-457-3230

www.winterspublishing.com

Library of Congress Control Number: 2005937646
ISBN 1-883651-25-5

Testimonials

What can you, a homemaker and/or mother, do when you do not know what to do? Yes, of course, read your Bible daily and pray many times during the day and night. Now you can also learn how to have victory over the circumstances from Mary Boyd Alley's "Meditations of a Happy Homemaker," a book too good to miss. Written from a caring heart for you, this experienced Godly wife and mother can help you to not only find peace in the midst of the storms of your life, but to also thank God for these stress-filled times.

Dr. Carolyn Diemer
President, Books Without Borders and author and illustrator
of "What the Bible Teaches About Life After Death"

ᏣᏲ

"Reading the reflections of my friend, Mary Boyd Alley, is like a spiritual visit into the deepest chambers of a virtuous woman's soul. Her warmth, wit, and wisdom have come to her through the channels of rich experience as a woman, a pastor's wife, a mother, a grandmother, and a dedicated follower of the Lord Jesus Christ. Her writing offers the best of Godly womanhood expressed with sympathy, strength, and colorful prose. For many years I have been challenged and encouraged through reading her thoughtful applications of Scripture to everyday life. It's my pleasure now to invite you to share with me – and with her – these lovely thoughts on the blessings of being a Christian woman."

Marilyn Boyer, author, conference speaker, and
mother to fourteen

Dedication

This book is dedicated to my Savior who made all good things possible for me.

I would also like to dedicate this book to my husband who has been encouraging in this project and to my five children, who gave me much to write about for over twenty years.

Table of Contents

PREFACE

It is a privilege and a pleasure to affirm the insights that Mary Boyd Alley possesses concerning women and their day to day burdens and blessings. Since I have lived with her for over 45 years, I have received an inside look at life decisions that sharpened her focus as they confirmed her convictions. As a first time mother, this college trained and experienced medical technologist chose the investment opportunity in the life of our firstborn over her profession. Later, she would give up typical dreams of prosperity common to most American homemakers, as she stood willingly with her husband in his belief that the leadership and prompting of God was to leave his profession of Pharmacy and to gain seminary training for special Christian ministry.

As a pastor's wife and as a missionary associate, she has grown from the post college girl to the mature laborer, mother of 5 children and grandmother of 9 grandchildren. In these transitions I have witnessed her increase in discernment concerning the challenges of womanhood. It has been a joy to also see her empathy for the single mother and the divorced woman as she grew in her perception of their burdens. Specific articles written will reflect an ability to distinguish between biblical womanhood and the humanist philosophy often labeled as feminism.

The analogies you read are simply Mary Boyd Alley's connections made out of the life experiences that have been both hers and those around her. Those 5 children have risen up to call her blessed. I hope you will also be blessed as you gain a small portion of encouragement from this lady who has been a great encourager to her life partner.

In grace and with gratitude,

Dr. Jim Alley

1

Who Said Housework, Done Right, Will Kill You?

❧

Hospitality

As I sautéed onions, peppers, and celery together while making dinner, I thought of a woman in an apartment building in the middle of Havana. My husband, his sister, and I visited Cuba in 2001 with another couple on a humanitarian objective. Mara is one of perhaps half a million people living in that crowded part of the city. The buildings are run down, but still many people inhabit whatever part of a building they can find. The woman we visited lived in a corner, with a bedroom containing a double bed, a crib, and one small table. That's all the space there was in the room. The other room, which had no door to separate it from the hall, had three broken chairs with a clothesline strung in front of them. Across from the chairs was her kitchen which consisted of a stone shelf. Under the shelf was a large sack of rice. On top of the shelf was a single burner attached to a tube running from a can hung on the wall with whatever fuel was available. The sink was a dishpan with water brought from the small bathroom. The Cuban woman lived in her cubbyhole about the size of our living room with five other people. Even when our children were all living at home, there were seven of us and seven rooms. No wonder we seem like rich Americans. While we visited, she began to cook a cupful of vegetables to flavor the rice. Just as we women here plan and cook supper for our family, she was doing the same thing. Their dinner might include rice and beans while ours may be fried chicken with potatoes and beans. There are cultural differences, but the home responsibilities are the same.

While the men and the missionary visited with a couple next door and gave them the gospel, we women visited with Mara. After a time, she rinsed two glasses with her hands with water from the little bathroom and poured us an orange drink. We drank it. She was giving us all she had for guests. Later, a medical doctor was quite concerned that we had drunk from glasses that were less than sanitary, but we felt we had to respect her hospitality. We are thankful we didn't seem to suffer any ill effects from the situation.

How would you like for a preacher to bring strangers from another country to see your home? If you had nothing else but what you were preparing for supper that night, would you have cheerfully shared a soda with strangers? Romans 12:13 says we are to be "given to hospitality." We read in I Peter 4:9, "Use hospitality one to another without grudging." Hospitality is sharing whatever we have for spiritual and physical refreshment of our guests. We have so much more than Mara in her little cubicle of a home, but she was a great example of hospitality in adverse circumstances. This incident reminded me to continue to use my home for hospitality whenever it is needed and not worry about whether everything is in order or not.

CR80

Home Cooking

We have planted, watered, weeded, and gathered, and now, at the end of summer, we enjoy the abundance of harvest from gardens, trees, and vines. God has promised to supply our needs (Philippians 4:19), but sometimes food is different according to geographical location and conditions.

Some southern foods that we love are country ham and biscuits, hoppin' John (black-eyed peas with rice), green beans cooked with new potatoes, and a plate of vine-ripened freshly sliced tomatoes. All week one summer I made damson jelly. For those of you who are not familiar with damsons, they are an oval purple plum of Syrian origin that grow well in this area and make marvelous jelly and preserves. Blackberries are also native to this region and are good for jelly or jam, cobblers, and jam cake.

This is not fast food, but slow food. This kind of food does not come from a can or take-out, but must be picked, washed, snapped, peeled, simmered, or mashed and dripped (for jelly). Unless one has "tame" (thornless) blackberries, one must tromp through weeds and get chiggers and scratches to pick blackberries, but they are soooo good, much better than store-bought jelly.

In the Mediterranean area when he offered them bread and fish, Jesus called his disciples to "Come and dine" (John 21:12). What a wonderful breakfast prepared by Jesus for his friends on the shores of the Sea of Tiberius or the Sea of Galilee. The children of Israel also feasted on a bountiful supply of manna in the wilderness. When they tired of manna and wanted meat, they asked, "Can God furnish a table in the wilderness?" (Psalm 78:19). God did just that – He gave them fresh water and meat.

One time when we had been invited to a Chinese New Year meal, we noticed that the food was not the same as what we ate in Chinese restaurants. When we inquired, the Chinese ladies told us what we would eat that day was "home cooking," and better, in their opinion, than what is served in "Chinese" restaurants. We all certainly do like our home cooking. We are thankful for the way God has made the earth to bring forth fruit. Although we are charged not to trust in uncertain riches, we are also assured in I Timothy 6:17 that "God ... gives us richly all things to enjoy." This must include ripe tomatoes, green beans, blackberries, damson plums, squash, cantaloupes, peppers, and onions. Yum, yum. I am getting hungry just writing about all the good things that grow in our garden.

༼ঙ৪ঙ༽

Tracks in the Carpet

When we had new, plush carpet put in a high traffic area in our home, it looked so nice and clean. There were no tracks, no footprints, no dirt in the new carpet the afternoon it was installed, and it smelled so good. Later, my husband walked across it. I looked at the new carpet, and lamented, "Now there are tracks in the carpet." He was not the least bit disturbed by the footprints he had just left. He simply said, "That's what happens to carpet; tracks will be in it."

Some fastidious homemakers may vacuum every day to prevent "tracks" in the carpet, but not I. I have been in houses where I was afraid to walk across the floor for fear of leaving telltale footprints. Our house is not like that. Many people besides our family will come into our home every year, and they will add to the normal wear of the carpet and house. That's fine with us, because we value our friends more than our possessions, at least I hope I do. It is good to keep a clean house so as to keep the sanitation department away, but a house also needs to be "dirty" enough to be comfortable.

Some of us get our lives in order and do not want anything to make "tracks" in our schedule. But life decrees that there are circumstances beyond our control that may change what we do and when. I am again learning flexibility in that my schedule occasionally is changed drastically. We do not plan to attend funerals, but we do. We do not plan to be sick, but we are sometimes. We do not like to rearrange meetings and conferences, but we do, and that's OK. We do not need to be so rigid that we cannot meet the needs of others when it affects our schedule.

In all these schedule changes and unexpected turn of events, we must trust in the Lord, who knows all things. Instead of "getting in a dither," as my mother used to say, I have begun to realize I am expendable. Someone else can do what I am doing, if necessary. We need to trust God to see us through when interruptions make tracks through our schedules or someone tries to "walk" on us. "Thou wilt keep him in perfect peace, whose mind is stayed on thee; because he trusteth in thee" (Isaiah 26:3).

ᓂᓂᓂ

Washing Windows

One time as I was in the house washing windows, the sun was beaming in my face. Even though it was uncomfortable, the brightness enabled me to see smears that otherwise might have been overlooked. When I stepped back, I was able to look out a clean window to get a clear view of what was on the other side. The blue sky and green grass and trees were more beautiful than they would have been if seen through gray, dirty windows.

At the same time I was also making a counted cross stitch item which says, "Let the beauty of Jesus be seen in me" to remind me that I need to let God work in my life so others may see Him, not me. Our lives, however, are like windows. If they are not clean, others may not see the beauty of Jesus in me. I cannot squirt something on my soul and wipe it off, but I must confess the sin in my life. Then I will be a clean vessel for the Master's use. "Having therefore these promises, dearly beloved, let us cleanse ourselves from all filthiness of the flesh and spirit, perfecting holiness in the fear of God" (II Corinthians 7:1). These are the obvious dirty spots in my life, like those on the windows. "Cleanse thou me from secret faults" (Psalm 19:12). These secret faults are revealed by the Word of God and are like the smears that show up on windows when the sun shines through that would be otherwise missed. I need to ferret out the secret sins that are not so obvious and may be hidden more deeply.

Although I do not clean windows as much as I probably should, I do get out the spray bottle and lint-free cloth and give it a swipe at regular intervals. When the windows are plainly dirty, I am more motivated to clean them. Sin separates between us and God and when it becomes apparent that is the problem, I finally get the picture and confess that sin. Let's "cleanse our hands ... and purify our hearts" (James 4:8) so we may be clean and transparent like just-washed windows. Then the beauty of Jesus may be seen in us. When you clean windows, think of the transparency we all need in our lives for Jesus to shine through.

CB&O

Mansions

At one time there were homebuilders in the United States who came up with a unique idea of not just building a house, but of completely furnishing it, right down to coordinating linen, china, and crystal. These million dollar homes were for the "newly rich" with plenty of money to spend, but not the time to choose furniture and accessories. I have not been in these million dollar homes, but the way home prices are escalating, I may see one soon. I have been in really gorgeous homes of friends. One couple with one child said they had nine bedrooms, and we could stay with them the next time we visited. I have been in one home with a built-in swimming pool in the middle of the home. Some large houses have mini-apartments for family members built into the home. Other people have offices or studios in addition to living room, dining room, kitchen, family room, laundry room, and several bedrooms. Lest you get the wrong idea, all my friends are not rich, but I have been invited into some really impressive homes.

Before we are tempted to be envious, remember the promise of Jesus in John 14: 2, 3. "In my Father's house are many mansions; if it were not so, I would have told you. I go to prepare a place for you. And if I go and prepare a place for you, I will come again, and receive you unto myself, that where I am, there ye may be also." Jesus has been preparing a place for us for almost two millennia that will be glorious beyond our wildest imagination. The mansions Jesus prepares will outdo and outshine anything I have described thus far.

Some of the differences in a millionaire's mansion and the heavenly mansion of believers are that one house cannot last nor bring happiness, but in the home Jesus prepares we will have eternal joy. One will be difficult to afford the upkeep and keep clean, while the other will be free for every believer. One will eventually wear out, but the other will last forever.

Our lot in life here may not always be comfortable, enjoyable, or pleasurable, but we have much to look forward to. When we read "Eye hath not seen, nor ear heard, neither have entered unto the heart of man, the things which God hath prepared for them that love him," (I Corinthians 2:9) our anticipation of heaven is heightened. That marvelous city of which we read in Revelation 21 will have the glory of God. There will be precious stones in the walls, gates and streets; the Lamb shall be the light of it; and there shall be no night there. What a glorious place to spend eternity, far surpassing any home on earth! But it is only for those who have put their faith and trust in the Lord Jesus Christ.

Readers, do you anticipate heaven? Will you have a heavenly mansion or is your earthly home all you will ever enjoy? With Jesus as your Savior, all these blessings of divinely prepared mansions will also be yours.

CRThO

Closets

Someone opened the door and reached for a rag and cleanser. There they are between the Band-Aids and the furniture polish. This shelf has assorted cleaning articles along with odds and ends. Out of season blankets, Christmas decorations, and various miscellaneous items inhabit the top shelf, while bed linens and beach towels stay on the bottom shelf.

My friend has clothes, shoes, scarves, polo shirts, handbags, and hats on her shelves and rods. A person may open the door, grab what she needs, put it on, and leave. The only time other people see my friend is when everything is color-coordinated, lined up, and neatly sorted into see-through boxes.

You, dear readers, have surmised by this time that I am a closet. I am tucked away in a corner of the house. The owners never show me off or invite visitors to enter my dark interior unless they are selling the house. I might feel neglected or inferior except that I know that I am an essential part of this household. All of you ladies should be thankful for each closet in your home. Many of our grandmothers did not have closets, but had to hang clothes on wooden pegs or in large, heavy armoires or wardrobes. These closets or silent servants keep the household running smoothly, as well as hide a multitude of items we do not wish to display.

What kind of servant are we? Do we want to be the kind that is exhibited with fanfare or not? Do we mind if others get credit for our work? Are we willing to hide a multitude of sins? Do we sometimes tend to feel used and unappreciated, but say nothing of it to anyone but the Lord? Can we say with the Psalmist, "O Lord, truly I am thy servant?" (Psalm 116:16). Are we able to stay in the background and work for God without experiencing resentment? Can we keep on going without much encouragement? "Blessed is that servant whom his lord, when he cometh, shall find so doing" (Luke 12:43).

I hope many of us are like the closet which is used without much attention being paid to it. May we be willing to be used of

God, knowing we are needed in our place, even though often we are an unappreciated servant. May we realize we are essential to the ongoing work of the Lord, but be willing to stay in the background and give all praise to God when anything good is accomplished.

෴

Home Decoration

One week I took all the pictures off the walls in one room and took curtains down in order to paint the room. The next week I washed the kitchen curtains. With bare walls and windows, a room seems cold and sterile. Even cut-rate motels have pictures attached to the wall to make the room a more comfortable place to spend the night. I know some men do not like for their wives to hang pictures because that means nail holes in the walls, but photographs, pictures, plaques, wall hangings, and curtains make a room cozier and more inviting. I think God made women to want to beautify our homes. We want to add a "woman's touch." The eye appreciates the aesthetic value of such decorations, and the ear does not hear the echo of sound bouncing off bare walls.

One does not need to invest in an expensive oil painting in order to warm up a room – a child's painting, an old quilt, or a great photograph made with a point-and-shoot camera in a garage sale frame will do. Accessories mean that we care about our home and want to make it say "Welcome" to those who enter. These little touches mean so much to family when they are made to feel "at ease" or comfortable in a home. The main objective of making our home an attractive haven is to give people a place to relax, unwind, and not be "uptight."

Just as I "fix up" my home, I must "fix up" my heart to welcome the Word of God by reading the Bible, memorizing and meditating on verses and passages I read. I am encouraged in

Colossians 3:16 to "Let the word of Christ dwell in you richly in all wisdom." The Greek word for *dwell* means "to inhabit," "to be at home" there. The Word of Christ should not just visit my life on Sunday when I go to church, but should be "at home" there every day. The Word of Christ must inhabit my heart and beautify it, like accessories make my home appealing.

Does the word of Christ inhabit your life? Is it "at home" in your heart surrounded by other familiar verses, or is your heart a bare, cold place for God's Word, bereft of any welcome decoration? Let's begin to renovate our hearts to receive the truth from the Lord as we redecorate our homes.

CRSO

Hands

A magazine article declared that hands are one of the most conspicuous parts of our body, and they are clues to age. There were instructions as to how to care for hands. Not only are we supposed to clean, file, and polish nails, but we should use an exfoliating hand mask (no, I don't know what that is), glycolic-acid and paraffin treatments, and hot oil soaks. A professional manicurist is also able to apply all these remedies to hands in a salon for you.

We women would all like to have beautiful hands and nails, but sometimes our hands are not in great shape because of the nature of our work. A mother may need to clean up a spill or change a diaper, play ball, or scrub floors, and not have time to put on rubber gloves or hand lotion with a high SPF. Some women do not have or use protection for hands when washing dishes, gardening, housework, or any of various chores that need to be done daily. A few women may have an executive position requiring little stress for their hands besides handling important papers and shaking the hands of important people, but most of us do the dirty work present in our jobs. Because of this and other factors, hands may have wrinkles, arthritis, dermatitis, or "horrid age-spots." If it seems that your grandmother's hands are peeking out from your sleeves, it's probably because you have been busy working.

The Bible says, "Whatsoever thy hand findeth to do, do it with thy might; for there is no work, nor device, nor knowledge, nor wisdom, in the grave, whither thou goest" (Ecclesiastes 9:10). We cannot stop diligently working at what the Lord has given us to do just for the appearance of our hands, because there will come a time when we cannot do our work. The grave may come too soon, and then it will be too late to work with our hands.

Our Creator has crafted our hands in such a way that we can do a myriad of tasks that will glorify Him. Other creatures in the animal kingdom cannot care for their young the way we can, nor produce art, nor eat, nor live in the same way. Animals are not able to write ideas onto a page of paper, which is one of the most significant of all ways of communicating. What a privilege we have to use our hands all the time in what God has given us to do. We must use these instruments of dexterity to do what has been placed before us in a way that will please our Lord and bring glory to Him.

CR80

Dishwashers and Dishcloths

Murphy's Law states that if anything can go wrong, it will go wrong at the worst possible time. Do you sometimes mutter that it's true while you try to rectify the situation? Isn't it frustrating to have the shaggiest lawn in the neighborhood when the lawn mower won't start? I heard about one woman who locked her keys in the car, which was still running, with her skirt caught in the car door, and it was raining! Wouldn't you be ready to give up? I would. I would stand in the parking lot and cry.

How do you feel when your dishwasher breaks and you are having a house full of guests for dinner the next day? That's what happened to me one Easter Sunday when there were almost more diners than my tables could accommodate, and I had to wash the dishes by hand! Actually, it's not that bad. I consider a dishwasher a luxury, although I have enjoyed using one for years, with a growing family and frequent dinner guests.

When something like this happens, it makes me stop and think of how much I have that I take for granted. Timothy tells us that "having food and raiment, let us be therewith content" (I Timothy 6:8). That means that a dishwasher, electric range, refrigerator, and many other appliances in my modern kitchen are really luxuries, things I can live without, if necessary. It also makes me extremely grateful for these silent servants in the culinary area.

When things go wrong or break down, I can learn contentment. It is expressed so well in a verse my mother had propped in her kitchen for years that puts things in perspective:

Thank God for dirty dishes.
They have a tale to tell.
By the ones we have before us
It seems we're doing well.
While folks abroad go hungry,
I haven't the heart to fuss,
For by the stack of evidence
God's very good to us.

Another lesson I have learned from dirty dishes is flexibility. We learn very quickly to go to plan B. I have a sink, soap and a dishcloth, so it is not a big problem to wash dishes. People all over the world do it every day.

Mark it down, something will go wrong this week. If you are doing anything at all, something frustrating is bound to happen.

When it does, try to look at it as something God can use to teach what He needs for you to know. If we realize God knows all about our circumstances and can use it to benefit our lives, it makes it easier to withstand any pressure a tense situation may bring.

అ৪৩

Entropy Reigns

In the course of our home education study, we came upon a unit involving thermodynamics. Thermodynamics is the study of the relation between heat and other forms of energy in physical and chemical processes. In the second law of thermodynamics, the term *entropy*, was introduced, which is a measure of the "disorder" or degradation in a system. Entropy increases unless an outside force uses energy to bring about order. Now this may sound complicated, but every good housewife and mother understands exactly what I am talking about. What has more energy than young, healthy children? (You may add pets.) What can make more clutter and track in more dirt than our precious offspring? Unless your child is a paragon of perfection, disorder is the rule.

One day after I had spent a great amount of time cleaning, vacuuming, mopping, dusting, and polishing, my children came skipping in the door, inadvertently taking some of the shine off my gleaming house. In response to my expression of frustration, my youngest child stopped, lifted his hand with a finger pointed skyward and declared with great authority in his voice, "Entropy reigns!" It was true then as well as now. My own little universe was becoming disorganized. A clean house is a temporary thing. So is everything man attempts.

Contrary to some popular opinions, mankind is not getting better and better. Those trying to get to heaven without Christ become less spiritual, not more spiritual, as they go through life. They become less grateful and more immoral. The last days are described in I Timothy 3:1-5. Mankind as a whole becomes worse, not better. Only a supernatural occurrence can reverse this process. This is the good news that we have to tell to the world. "Christ Jesus came into the world to save sinners" (I Timothy 1:15). We need to reach men and women, boys and girls, before they get older and become hardened to the gospel when disorder will reign in their hearts.

Let's not let entropy reign in our spiritual lives. Let's get our own lives in order by godly discipline so we may reach others for Christ. More and more people are moving in disorderly fashion toward the edge, into the abyss prepared for the devil and his angels. We can put a stop to it. It will require energy to interject the gospel into the lives of others, but we must do it.

ଔୄ

Quilts

Quilts are fascinating items of needlework. At a quilt show, a county or state fair, or in a person's home who has several quilts, one may be overwhelmed by the quality, quantity, and ingenuity of the quilts displayed. Even when quilters use the same pattern, no two quilts are alike. From pieced quilts to appliquéd, embroidered, or trapunto, these quilts represent much thought and literally thousands of hours of handwork. Whether made from old blue jeans or the newest calico, each quilt is unique in its beauty and style.

Just like quilts, each person is a unique individual who was made by God for the praise of His glory. The Psalmist tells us "it is He that hath made us, and not we ourselves" (Psalm 100:3), and that "I am fearfully and wonderfully made" (Psalm 139:14). God created each one of us different from all others – we are one of a kind. God also says that we are precious to Him, and He loves us. "Thou wast precious in my sight . . . I have loved thee" (Isaiah 43:4).

Quilts are precious to their makers because of the time spent in planning, cutting and stitching. Each quilt is cut from different material, and pieced together in a different way from all others. One quilt may be made from three or four colors of fabric sewn in a precise design to coordinate with a certain color scheme. Another may be fashioned from anything available in a haphazard manner to make a "crazy quilt." Both are pleasing and useful in their own way.

Christians may look different from each other, not dress alike, and speak with their own regional accent or language, but all can be pleasing to the Father and useful in the Kingdom. Just as prize-winning quilts bring blue ribbons to their makers, so we can also bring glory to our heavenly Father. We can each be useful and pleasing to the Father even though we are different from other people. Each person is an individual who is loved by God. We should also love and accept each individual person as God does.

A quilter must be careful to cut each piece straight and seam it true. In shops I have seen quilts that looked so beautiful until I was close enough to see the handwork on it. It seemed to me it was hurriedly quilted, and the price reflected that. A child learning to quilt will not have the small stitches of a seasoned quilter that make the quilt more valuable. These quilts are not perfect, but the quilting would probably not be noticed by anyone but a good seamstress.

Instead of focusing on our differences and coveting someone else's talents, gifts, or good fortune, we should be bringing honor to the Lord in our own unique way. Because of sin, we are not perfect either, but we do fit into God's eternal plan. We cannot afford to waste time worrying over trivial things. Yes, we should confess sin and be forgiven, but then we should move on to serve the Lord.

It is imperative that a quilter work precisely to render a finished product that fits together, but we cannot spend time trimming each tiny piece if the whole square finally works out. We must also discipline ourselves not to spend an inordinate amount of time on trifling entities, but direct our energies to accomplish God's will for our own lives. Then we will form a pleasing pattern of loveliness that will attract others to the Lord.

There is a box of fabric remnants carefully stacked for me to go through to choose the material for a new quilt. I can't wait to see the beautiful design that will emerge from scraps to the finished product. Happy quilting to you ladies.

∽∾

Company's Coming

Frequently, we will have a visiting speaker for our Sunday morning services, and he and his wife will be staying with us. While it does not take a great amount of effort to prepare for two extra people, I will do a little more than usual in the way of cooking and house cleaning. We have had as many as 13 people sleep at our house at one time, but more often, it is only one person or a family of four or five. Our meals will increase to accommodate four or seven instead of two, and I will make sure the house is clean, the bathroom is sparkling, and there are extra towels available. Then we will enjoy our company.

Sometimes, however, we work ourselves into a frenzy thinking about someone coming to our home. We want everything to be perfect. We want our home to look like it is ready to be photographed for a national interior decorating magazine. Why? Because we feel that anything less is a negative reflection on us. I used to be like that, but not anymore. I am not the world's best housekeeper; I admit it. If I waxed floors, cooked gourmet meals, washed windows, and shampooed carpets, in addition to the regular cleaning in anticipation of the arrival of guests, I would be too exhausted to enjoy fellowship with my friends. They might also think I maintained an impeccable home all the time, which just isn't true. Again, I want to have a clean, neat, warm home, but without seeming to be faultless.

Now think what it would be like if Jesus came to our houses. If he dropped by unexpectedly, would we have to scramble to scoop up trashy novels and candy wrappers? Would we quickly have to stuff the contents of our cupboards and refrigerator in the garbage can? Would we cringe at the greeting and conversation with which our children would meet him? Would we want to change clothes? Would we dash to turn off the television set before answering the door? For those of us who are Christians, the Lord knows all about us anyway and would not be impressed with any kind of facade we might try to project. The most important question for us wives and mothers, homemakers, is are we using our talents and energy to cheerfully share our food, our homes, and ourselves with those God brings into our life?

"Be not forgetful to entertain strangers; for thereby some have entertained angels unawares" (Hebrews 13:2).

" ... given to hospitality" (Romans 12:13).

෪෨

Spring Cleaning

When my husband decides it is warm enough not to use our wood stove, I try to start spring cleaning. I know you may have done this before late spring, just as I have, but I begin as soon as I have time for in-depth cleaning. I start in the kitchen by taking everything out of the cupboards and cabinets, relining shelves with new paper, and putting it all back. In carrying out this process, I found one item that had been pushed so far back it was no longer usable; its shelf life had expired. This thing had to be thrown out. Most cans, packages, and condiments just had to be checked and put back. It is a lot of work, but it gives a feeling of accomplishment when finished.

It occurred to me in cleaning house, that this would be a good time to clean my spiritual "house," and the time preceding, during, and following a revival meeting would be the perfect time to take a spiritual inventory. Periodically I should take stock of myself spiritually. I need to ask, "Am I as close to the Lord as in the past?" or "Am I harboring any bitterness or resentment toward anyone and have not tried to deal with it?" or "Is God trying to get my attention to tell me something, and I am not ready to listen?" I don't think God would ask something of us beyond our capabilities. Of course, we can do nothing in our own strength anyway; we must rely on Him. The Apostle Paul said, "I can do all things through Christ which strengtheneth me" (Philippians 4:13).

As we take out attitudes for examination, some like hypocrisy, greed, and pride have been in our hearts too long and need to be thrown out by resistance and rebuke. Other attitudes such as kindness, gentleness, love, tolerance, and gratefulness need to be dusted off and put in a prominent place in our lives so they are ready for frequent use.

As I take stock of my life, I know God is reasonable in His expectations. He knows we are but flesh, so He has made it simple for us. We read in Micah 6:8, "He hath shewed thee, O man, what is good; and what doth the Lord require of thee, but to do justly, and to love mercy, and to walk humbly with thy God?" If I can do that, I will do what I should. If I walk humbly with God, I will have a good spiritual inventory. Because of Christ's death and resurrection, "the righteousness of the law might be fulfilled in us, who walk not after the flesh, but after the spirit" (Romans 8:4).

As you clean out those cupboards and drawers, and scrub those walls and floors, remember we are to be clean vessels fit for the Master's use. "Who shall stand in his holy place? He that hath clean hands, and a pure heart" (Psalm 24:3, 4).

Ladies, doesn't it feel good to know all the musty corners in your kitchen are clean and ready for more efficient meal preparation? Doesn't it feel good to know your house is spotless and ready for company? It feels good, too, to know we have gotten our hearts right with God and are ready to serve Him by serving others. Once kitchens or hearts are clean it is much easier to keep both in "apple pie" order. As we confess our sins and claim God's promises, we are on our way to a life of holiness. "Having, therefore, these promises, dearly beloved, let us cleanse ourselves from all filthiness of the flesh and spirit, perfecting holiness in the fear of the Lord" (II Corinthians 7:1).

CRID

Ants

After a storm in which many trees were blown down, creepy-crawly creatures sought refuge in our homes when theirs were wrecked. The warm, humid weather also brought bugs indoors. One morning I was greeted by a steady stream of tiny ants to and from a minuscule crumb in the sink that had inadvertently been left overnight. After I cleaned the sink, counters and obliterated all the ants' scent trails, I thought we were clear – especially when my husband sprinkled a high-powered bug killer all around the house. A few days later when we had guests, a plate with a piece of dessert was set down close to a window, and within minutes an army of ants was attacking the sweet stuff. There were no ants anywhere else, but, of course, I was chagrined to think they were on a guest's plate.

The invasion of these little ants is like the entrance of sin in our lives. The small sins, like the ants, are subtle and inconspicuous at first. A soft choice at one point may lead to indulgence and greed later.

The Bible mentions ants twice in the book of Proverbs in

6:6-8 and 30:25. In both instances I learned that these pests are industrious. By observation I have seen that they are cooperative, too. They quickly find food, relay the information to other members of their nest, set up a trail others can follow and bring back their prize. Sin, too, wastes no time in setting up a system to get in, irritate, take over, and destroy our lives if left unchecked.

To get rid of ants, we must deny them access to our houses or destroy their nests. If we cannot find the place where they come in, we must leave no food out for ants to eat. That means rinsing food containers, storing pet food dishes where ants cannot get to them, washing dishes and keeping counters clean.

In the same way we must remove the welcome mat for sin by asking, "What is its point of entry for me?" When that is identified, I can seal up this weakness with the Word of God and prayer.

Ladies, I hope you haven't experienced this same problem with ants or sin, but if you have, be alert to "every weight, and the sin which doth so easily beset us" and look to Jesus that we "may serve God acceptably with reverence and godly fear" (Hebrews 12:1, 28). This doesn't mean we will be without sin, but that there is a way to deal with it through confession. If we keep our lives and homes clean, neither sin nor ants will be able to get a foothold and we can live without fear of these things.

CRUD

The Clothesline

In contrast to past summers in our neighborhood when the weather has warmed, there are several clotheslines now firmly anchoring the sails of freshly laundered garments to their terrestrial sea. I wonder if, perhaps, other housewives have discovered the secret of the clothesline.

Many people do not hang clothes out for lack of time or energy or the neighborhood in which they live won't allow it. I hang clothes out and save my dryer for rainy or snowy days. Another plus is that the clothes smell so fresh. At the clothesline I am out of hearing distance of the telephone. I like to communicate with friends, but I am annoyed with sales pitches, wrong numbers, and so forth. As I use my solar-powered clothes dryer, I am saving electricity as well as getting exercise and fresh air. No one asks, "I'm bored, can Billy come play?" or "Can we split a Pepsi or get on the internet?" If a child comes to the clothesline with a question of that nature, he knows he will be put to work hanging up clothes. Another advantage is that I can use that time to plan other activities of the day, or for peaceful meditation.

A clothesline is just one of the benefits of being a homemaker. Those of us who have chosen to stay at home should enjoy the blessings we have. We are told in Proverbs 14:23 that "In all labor there is profit." We can use the time and skills we have at hand to be of profit to our families.

One summer after four consecutive days of rainy, damp weather, the sun finally appeared and a breeze was stirring enough to hang clothes outside again to dry. When I arrived at the clothesline, I discovered that all my clothespins had been left out in the humid weather, and all were partially or fully covered with black mold. I mean they were fuzzy! What do you do with two loads of clean clothes and dirty clothespins? I dumped the clothespins in the laundry room sink, poured bleach on them and let them soak a while. Then I rinsed them and hung them on the line to dry in the sun. In an hour some of the stains were still there, but the organisms that caused the mold were gone and could not be transferred to the clean clothes. When completely dry, most of the clothespins were almost like new.

Sometimes we wander for a period of time in the wrong spiritual atmosphere. We get away from reading God's Word and prayer. When we get out from under the divine protection of God's love and become indifferent to spiritual things, we become defiled just as the mold and mildew grew on my wooden clothespins. We then need to go through a similar procedure to be cleansed. We need to go to the Word of God and be cleansed "with the washing of water by the word," (Ephesians 5:26) and walk in the light of fellowship with Christ. "But if we walk in the light as he is in the light, we have fellowship one with another, and the blood of Jesus Christ his Son cleanseth us from all sin" (I John 1:7). The results of sin are still with us, like the stains on the clothespins, but the forgiveness of sin can be enjoyed by the one who comes to the Word for cleansing and walks in the light, the "Sonlight."

Ladies, clean clothes are necessary for our families. Please do not feel you are wasting your time or brainpower in this activity. Nineteenth century preacher, teacher, and writer, Richard Baxter said, "Spend your time in nothing which you know must be repented of; in nothing on which you might not pray for the blessing of God; in nothing in which you could not review with a quiet conscience on your dying bed; in nothing in which you might not safely and properly be found doing if death should surprise you in the act." This should apply to all our activities, whether we have multiple ministries outside the home or are at home moms with household duties … including hanging out clothes.

C3&0

Home

Vacations are a time for a change of scenery and schedules. It is a time to relax, unwind, and "get away from it all." Vacations can be very important times of refreshment. Many people could vacation for a month at a time or more and enjoy it immensely, while others cannot be away from the phone or business for longer than a day.

Like others, I also like to see friends, loved ones, and new places, but traveling extensively and living out of a suitcase is not for me . . . at least not for long periods of time. I do travel frequently with my husband on mission trips, but I do like to be in my own home, hang clothes in my closet, sleep in my own bed, use my own pillow, and be in familiar territory. I had rather open the windows at night and hear crickets and night sounds than the hum of an air-conditioner. I am just a "homebody."

People are different and some would travel all the time if possible. My mother used to say of a friend that she could have been a cross-country truck driver because she always liked to be on the go. If you like to be at home like I do, we cannot settle down too much. If God should call us to another geographical location, we must be ready to move. We should look forward to a new challenge instead of worrying about being uprooted. We must be ready to go at the sound of the heavenly trumpet (I Thessalonians 4:16, 17). We are strangers and pilgrims here on earth just as the Old Testament patriarchs were (Hebrews 11:13).

Ladies, let's keep our homes (Titus 2:5) and make them a haven from the world. I think too often we become entrenched in our homes and want to keep the world out and just enjoy ourselves in our little nest. Our homes are for keeping at bay the cares of the world, but we should be willing to share what we have with others who need a quiet resting place without the distraction of the world. Let's make our homes a place of fun and ease for our families – even a place where we can relax from the wearisome travels of a vacation. But let's not forget that this is only a temporary place of habitation. Our final home is in heaven.

03800

2

Children are an Heritage of the Lord . . . and Sometimes a Handful for Mom

૦૩૮૦

Hats Off to Mothers!

Many years ago on a cold February day, I became a mother with the birth of my first child. He was so amazingly perfect a baby, and we were awed as new parents to see him grow and develop. What did I know about being a mother? Virtually nothing. I had a mother, and my mother had another baby, my sister, when I was 11, and I had held newborn babies in the hospital nurseries, but that was the extent of my experience with babies - especially tiny new babies.

Does God make the female of the species instinctively know how to care for their young? Yes, I think to a certain extent He does, but for human babies, God requires more rearing than for animals. He has made us social beings that we may help one another. I am thankful for a good example in my mother, as well as helpful neighbors and friends in various locations and towns where we lived. I observed other new mothers, and some not so new mothers in my young years, to try to gather wisdom in child-training. I also read books and talked to other women. We would sometimes get together to work out mutual problems of this important job.

We all naturally look to others to define our own roles, so I am glad for biblical illustrations, too. Eve, of course, was the mother of all living (Genesis 3:20). Moses' mother, of the tribe of Levi, was the courageous woman who hid her son from the king's wrath so he could grow up to be a national leader. David's great-grandmother had a book of the Bible named for her - Ruth. Hannah prayed for her son (I Samuel 1:27), and Solomon's mother taught him what a virtuous woman is in Proverbs 31. Mary the mother of Jesus served God well under difficult circumstances (Matthew 2:11). The mother of John Mark invited all her friends to pray in her house fervently enough to effect Peter's release from prison (Acts 12:12). The apostle Paul gave us many good instructions while mentioning Timothy's mother, Eunice and his grandmother, Lois (II Timothy 1:5).

In all this time and with all these wonderful examples, I, like most mothers, want my children to be happy, secure, and productive. Much of this is summed up in III John 4, "I have no greater joy than to hear that my children walk in truth."

Hats off to mothers everywhere who are doing a superb job of child-rearing. I applaud you who have hyperactive children or handicapped children and are still doing a great job with patience. I think highly of each mother who stays home to care for her children, instead of entering the workforce to fulfill herself, leaving her children in the care of others, as well as those mothers who, of necessity, have to work to provide for their children. I am extremely thankful for all those who have been an example for me over the years. I admire all those incredible women who reared children who turned out to be productive citizens of our community, as well as servants of the Lord. Congratulations on a job well done.

CRXO

The Ideal Mother

We all know who the perfect mother is because we have all conjured up images in our minds that describe her. The perfect mother is thrilled to know she will soon have a precious baby. Her baby sleeps most of the time except when he needs to be fed. As a toddler he learns the alphabet, colors, numbers, and can read before he starts to kindergarten. In elementary school, the perfect mother's child has perfect attendance and top grades, and he has memorized more Bible verses than anyone else in Sunday School. In high school, he excels in sports and academics, which open doors to many prestigious colleges and universities. This perfect offspring of perfect parents graduates from college with highest honors, gets a top job, marries, and produces perfect grandchildren.

Sounds good, doesn't it? Unfortunately, it does not sound real, either. Reality sometimes begins with morning sickness, months of discomfort, and a colicky baby. A good mother may have a child with physical problems or a learning disability that hinders schoolwork. A good mother spends much time in prayer for her children. She has a lap that welcomes a child that needs comfort. God says, "As one whom his mother comforteth, so will I comfort you" (Isaiah 66:13). No make-up can cover the sags and wrinkles that result from lack of sleep from staying up with a sick child or waiting for a wayward teen. A good mother makes cupcakes or a costume for school, although she only found out about the special occasion the night before.

The ideal mother may not have neatly manicured hands because she may pull weeds out of the garden so the vegetables will feed her growing family. She may break a fingernail throwing a baseball or a frisbee with her children. "She worketh willingly with her hands" (Proverbs 31:13). This mother wants a new sofa for the living room, but that money was spent on music lessons, basketball shoes, or a new baseball glove.

However, this mother does not feel that she is a martyr to

her children. She finds time to spend alone with her husband, and she reads, sews, paints, or exercises for her own pleasure. If she has no husband, she cultivates friends to share her burdens and joys. And makeup cannot hide the laugh lines that come from years of family jokes in a house that rings with laughter. "A merry heart maketh a cheerful countenance" (Proverbs 15:13).

The good mother does not have everything together. She knows the physical weariness that grips her body after months of dealing with a serious illness. She knows the emotional bleakness of financial strain or a runaway child. She knows the hurt of gossip that finally gets back to her. She knows the enormous sense of loss after a miscarriage or death of a child. And yet, in spite of the difficulties, this good mother doggedly hangs on to her family, her sanity, and her hope that one day it all will be worth it. "A woman that feareth the Lord, she shall be praised" (Proverbs 31:30).

Motherhood has its rewards, and we do not have to wait twenty or thirty years to see them. A reward may come in the form of sticky hands on the side of your face as a toddler looks at you in the eyes and coos, "I wuv oo, Mommy," or brings you a bouquet of dandelions. It may be a shy but sincere, "Thanks, Mom," from a middle-schooler suddenly realizing he forgot his lunch, when you thrust a brown bag in his hand as he heads for school. It may be a teenager who spends her babysitting money to buy you a flower arrangement for your birthday instead of more gaudy jewelry for herself. It may be a twenty-year-old who comes home to do his laundry. ("That's a reward for all my labor?" you may ask. Hey, he could be doing his laundry in his girlfriend's apartment!) "Her children rise up and call her blessed" (Proverbs 31:28).

The ideal mother and her ideal children exist only in our imaginations. But plenty of good mothers exist in reality. In this real world, you are the "ideal" mother for your children.

C33⬥80

The Sum of Motherhood

Is the sum of motherhood in the cards, flowers, or gifts we receive for Mother's Day? These things are nice, but motherhood is so much more. Motherhood is realized before the flutter of life is felt in the womb. The pain and travail of childbirth are forgotten as we see the tiny person entrusted to us by the God of Creation. Part of motherhood is kissing "owies," soothing the fevered brow, mopping up muddy footprints on a newly washed kitchen floor, and answering enigmatic questions. Motherhood is reading to, playing with, teaching, training, encouraging, modeling, and praying for and with our children, then backing off to let them make their own choices.

All the T-ball, basketball, soccer, softball, and volleyball games we have attended, all the art work on our refrigerators, all the bicycles, toys and dolls we have bought, all the bills from the orthodontist, orthopedist, music teachers, sports supply stores, and grocery stores, and all the hours we have waited to hear the family car in the driveway late at night, will be worth it as we see our sons and daughters stand tall and march into the world with a quiet confidence.

Sometimes we feel overwhelmed, tired, helpless. I have felt that way and longed for an escape, but having no way out, I stayed with this incredibly hard job. At times like this, I had to remind myself no one else is as concerned about my children as I am. I had to remember that I was not wasting my time by staying home with my children and not pursuing a career, though I am trained as a medical technologist. It seemed that I was "spinning my wheels" many times, but I had to have the faith that the investment in the early years of my children would eventually pay great dividends.

Much is expected of mothers today. Well-adjusted, honest, loving children don't just happen, but they are the result of many hours of facing trials with determination, a tough job with confidence borne of sleepless nights spent in prayer, and days of Scripture searches, as well as good, solid work as a parent. Motherhood can not be discounted or devalued because mothers, for the most part, are the ones who shape the lives and attitudes of their children. Mothers give emotional security to their children by nurturing their spirit and leading each one in the way God has gifted him.

Motherhood is knowing these precious souls we have tried to send forth as straight arrows, polished and true, will take our values into the future. My deepest longings and fulfillment will have been met if I have done my best to rear my children in the nurture and admonition of the Lord and to see them live these truths in the world.

Yes, motherhood is a vital, complex, and challenging duty, but women are especially suited for this rewarding occupation. Keep up the good work, mothers.

"Her children arise up, and call her blessed" (Proverbs 31:28).

CRUD

A Mother's Heart

On a summer evening after supper, at dusk when the air is still, the day has cooled down and the last afterglow remains, I sit in the backyard and remember. I think of the apple tree we planted between the pitcher's mound and home base for whiffle ball games. (The children could really whack a whiffle ball without losing it in the neighbor's yard like they would a baseball.) I think of two boys digging in the dust making roads for their cars. When I hear the peepers before the bull frogs add their bass to the harmony of nature's chorus, I remember a seven-year-old who caught his first fish and ran to show me. I remember a little girl who climbed trees and planted strawberries in that same backyard. Then I remember the changes of seasons, and sled tracks down the small hill behind our house, and a pine-scented igloo with two rooms built from the snow of a shoveled driveway. As I sit and swing, I think of all my children scattered in two continents and two states. I miss my children.

The nights of getting up with a newborn for 2 AM feedings, the "terrible twos" of toddlerhood, the first day of school, the turbulent teen years, and graduation from high school (which came too soon), are all part of life and growing up for them and for me. When they left for college, I realized what I thought was a hectic time was really the best time of my life. Young mothers, enjoy your children now. Enjoy every stage. Don't wish they would grow up . . . they will soon enough. I no longer have to cook gargantuan meals every night, or stock milk by the gallons, or juggle anyone else's schedule. I am no longer a "soccer mom." I seem to have plenty to keep me busy, but it's a different busy.

I wonder how God felt when his Son left heaven to come to live here. Jesus left the glorious place of heaven to live as a pauper in a dusty land and walk among us. Even though Jesus was doing the Father's will, he was away for awhile. Even though the redemption of the world had been planned, it must have wrenched the Father's heart to see the suffering of His Son, bearing the sins of the world. I'm sure God understands all we mothers go through with our children, even when the children are away from home temporarily or have left for good. "For God so loved the world, that he gave his only begotten Son, that whosoever believeth in him should not perish, but have everlasting life" (John 3:16).

Someday you young mothers will reminisce about the good days when your children were young and at home, even though you felt like a juggler trying to fit it all in. You older mothers, please remember the good times and forget the difficulties as you still "mother" your grown children. Let's thank God for the privilege of being mothers.

CR80

Babies

"Lo, children are an heritage of the Lord: and the fruit of the womb is his reward" (Psalm 127:3). On a Friday in July 1996, I received a phone call at church where I was working with Vacation Bible School. My daughter called to tell us she had given birth to a baby girl named Aimee Katherine. We were excited and rushed to tell anyone who would listen. Isn't it wonderful to be a grandmother!

Before we saw Aimee, we knew a little about new babies. New babies sleep, cry, and need to be fed, cleaned, and held. They cannot do anything for themselves. We still love them when they smell bad, sleep when we want to play with them, and are awake when we want to sleep so badly we can barely hold our own head up. We love to gaze at a baby and speculate whether she looks like Mom or Dad or great aunt Agnes. These tiny creations really get tangled around our hearts when we see that first smile that is a response, not a reaction to some internal twinge.

The next stage is when a baby is a few months old and is crawling, walking, and getting into everything. We walk miles bending over someone two feet tall whose little hands grasp our fingers. We try to get out of their mouths whatever they found on the floor or under furniture to determine if the object is harmful. Within two years this child will learn a foreign language - English, a very difficult language, but one that is mastered by this small person in an incredible time. We spend weeks trying to get a child to say "Mama," then weeks trying to get away from it, wishing she had an "off" switch or at least a button so we could turn down the volume.

We love these children who are so dependent on us and who need us so much. Yet, we will never be satisfied with them the way they are. We are not satisfied with a baby who only sleeps, eats, and makes messes. We want that baby to smile, talk, walk, play, learn to read and write, and grow up. We want that new baby to mature in the normal way.

A new Christian is much like a new baby. He or she has so much to learn about this new life and is quite dependent on others for his sustenance. A new Christian needs to feed on the milk of the Word of God. "As newborn babes, desire the sincere milk of the word, that ye may grow thereby" (I Peter 2:2). We should show them how to start reading in the Bible. A new Christian needs to learn how to walk. "We walk by faith, not by sight" (II Corinthians 5:7). "Walk in the Spirit, and ye shall not fulfill the lust of the flesh" (Galatians 5:16). "Walk in love" (Ephesians 5:2). "Walk in wisdom" (Colossians 4:5). " ... walk worthy of God ... " (I Thessalonians 2:12). A new Christian needs to know how to talk. "But speaking the truth in love ... Let no corrupt communication proceed out of your mouth ... Let all bitterness, and wrath, and anger, and clamor, and evil speaking be put away from you, with all malice" (Ephesians 4:15, 29, 31). A new Christian needs to learn to behave properly. "And be ye kind one to another, tender-hearted, forgiving one another ... " (Ephesians 4:32). "Be kindly affectioned one to another ... not slothful in business, rejoicing ... patient ... prayerful ... distributing to the necessity of saints, given to hospitality, Bless them which persecute you" (Romans 12:10-14).

This wise counsel from the Word of God will help all of us to grow up. Our sweet little babies naturally grow up so quickly. Let's not be so slow to grow as Christians.

CRSO

Choose Your League

A mother of several very young children related an incident in which she felt a twinge of envy in the presence of another woman who was a rising professional person. The professional woman was dressed attractively in a business suit with her briefcase, perfectly coifed, and quite articulate. The mother thought, "I have a college degree and could pursue a career, but I have chosen to have children and train them to love and serve the Lord." In my opinion, the mother made a wise choice and dealt with the situation in a mature way. When her children are older, she may choose to pursue a career.

Each of us makes choices that affect many people close to us, as well as the direction of our lives. A mother of toddlers or young children cannot keep a house as clean and neat as a mother whose children are grown and away from home. The younger mother is in a younger league, and there should not be a sense of competition. Sometimes as we scrub and vacuum, we find ourselves wishing for a maid. We are not content to stay in the minor leagues until later.

Several years ago I met a woman named Martha, who said she wondered if she had been named Mary if she would have had so much housework, referring to the story of Jesus and the sisters of Bethany in Luke 10. I immediately assured her that, since my name was Mary, it would not matter; a woman's work is never done! Jesus, knowing all about Martha's anxiety, still said, "Mary hath chosen that good part."

Many of you younger women may feel like you are stuck in the minor leagues. You may feel like you have chosen to stay at home, but you are tired of the diaper bag and bottle routine and would like to talk to another adult more often than you do. Those of us with older children can tell you we have been there, and this will pass. However certain it may seem now, you will not have to send a bottle in your child's lunch box, nor will he wear diapers to school. You have chosen your league. Now, do as Mary and choose that good part of letting the Lord lead you through this phase of motherhood, too. You can "have it all," but you can't have it all at once.

CB80

Motherhood

"Take-Your-Daughter-to-Work Day" was begun to show girls what moms and dads do in a chosen field or occupation. Some girls may have been bored at a parent's workplace or she may have really liked it and want to follow in Mom's footsteps. In any case, girls learn what their mothers do all day. Mother's Day honors and gives respect to motherhood. Some mothers were ignored on Mother's Day, while others received flowers, candy, hugs, and kisses. What have our daughters (or our sons for that matter) learned about motherhood? Whatever happened on Mother's Day or in the workplace when daughters went with their moms to work, we all realize we would not be where we are now without Mom. (Is that why a hulking athlete grins and says, "Hi, Mom," when a TV camera zeros in on him?)

Those of us who are fortunate enough to be able to stay home with our children and be full-time homemakers know the contentment of being where we are needed. We know the satisfaction of teaching a five-year-old to tie shoes or of showing a teen how to cook. We see the wonder in a toddler's eyes at each new discovery even as we try to keep tiny curious hands out of danger. Then, as we guide our last teen through high school and on to college, we finally have time to take a breather from the frantic child-rearing years to reflect on motherhood ourselves.

We may not have extra money for concerts, but listening to endless scales and songs on a piano or violin or trumpet are a concert to our ears. Our working clothes may not be designer fashions, but our children think we are beautiful in whatever we wear because we are known as "Mom." Many women work because of necessity or by choice, and this is not to say they are not just as good mothers as those who are home all the time.

In the final analysis, our self-esteem, our affirmation as women, our completeness as a person comes not from our children and their accomplishments, but from a right relationship with God and in doing His will. The Lord created each of us with certain characteristics, and when we fulfill that for which we are created, our life will have a joy and peace that comes from no other source. God, and God alone, can satisfy the deepest needs of our hearts and make us radiant Christians who glorify Him whether we are mothers who stay at home, work, or wish for children. Motherhood is a high calling and those who rear godly children will be blessed and rewarded.

CR80

Child-like Trust

Children do not worry about what they are going to eat, how they will get to school or back home, when they have to get up or go to bed, or anything else. Children don't worry about how they are going to live or who will provide for them. They are children, and they know that we, as parents and grandparents, will take good care of them. The most concern of most children is whether they will have time to play with the toys they cherish, or whether they will be able to eat the tasty goodies they want.

When I start to worry about things, I need to remember how children trust in responsible adults to care for them. This is how God wants us to trust in Him. Our Lord has promised to give us everything we need at the present time. "But my God shall supply all your need according to His riches in glory by Christ Jesus" (Philippians 4:19). This promise tells us that God gives *according to* His riches, not *out from* His riches. If God gave us out from His riches, they would be depleted as we ask for more and more. As it is, God can give us as much as He deems fit and still have as much left for someone else.

We can sleep in peace knowing God is watching over us. " ... He that keepeth thee will not slumber. Behold, he that keepeth Israel shall neither slumber nor sleep" (Psalm 121:3, 4). We can sleep like a baby since God is in charge of the universe.

I just need to remember that I am not in control of the world and leave all those worries with our heavenly Father.

Where is our next meal coming from? We may not know, but we can ask for our food each day. "Give us this day our daily bread" (Matthew 6:11). We tend to stock our freezers and pantries with enough food to last for a long time instead of trusting God to provide each meal. If we had no refrigeration and had to go to market every day like people in other countries, we might learn to trust more.

We have much to teach our children during the brief time they are in our care, but we can learn from them at the same time as we observe their trust in us. Just look at a playground full of children. Do they seem anxious about their next meal or what they will wear the next day? No. Do they worry about having a home to go to? No. They trust that their parents will provide everything they need. Parents, we do need to provide nourishing meals, adequate, appropriate clothing for our children, and proper housing, but we also need to give them spiritual food. We can also teach Bible verses and let them see how we apply Bible principles to our everyday lives. "Train up a child in the way he should go" (Proverbs 22:6). Each child may be headed in a different direction, but it is up to us, as parents, to sort these things out and train the child accordingly.

Let's learn to trust in God like our children trust in us to provide whatever they need. It may not be everything they want, but we will supply their needs. This exercise will alleviate worry, help us to grow in faith and glorify the Lord all at the same time.

CR80

Do We Really Love Our Children?

Love is meeting a person's real needs, and a baby has real needs. Babies must be loved, fed, changed, kept warm, cuddled, and clothed. Most of us can adequately handle these basic requirements. We know children need love and not material things, but many parents now are spending record amounts of money on their children, especially first-time parents of infants. Many parents are waiting longer to have children and spending more on those babies to be sure they have cribs, car seats, food, formula, diapers, lotion, doctor's visits, shots, designer clothing, and little rubber coated baby spoons. Not only the basics, but a mind-boggling array of baby products is available for two-income families with more discretionary income to spend. A new parent can buy a name brand silver barbell rattle for Junior for $275, or a silver baby cup for $140, or a three-inch Waterford crystal baby block for $69. (Will it bother that parent when Junior throws the crystal block out of his crib, and it shatters into thousands of fragments?) Is this what our children really need?

Please do not feel bad if you can not afford to outfit your eight-month-old with a baby bunny silver bracelet for almost $200. Does your five-year-old really need a Lilly Pulitzer designer dress? What our children need are not expensive child accouterments, but to be brought up in the nurture and admonition of the Lord (Ephesians 6:4). Infants can be trained to be attentive to their parent's voice. This attentiveness can gradually be used to train the child to obedience, which is one of the most important character qualities a child can learn. A patient parent who teaches obedience is less likely to have a stubborn child. A child who learns obedience at home will be able to get along with other authorities such as teachers and employers later in their life.

Young mothers, do not fail to teach and train your children for the glory of God. Twenty years from now it will not matter if he wore designer diapers, but it will matter if he can properly relate to those around him and to God. Early training now will spare you many heartaches in future years. "Train up a child in the way he should go" (Proverbs 22:6).

CʒBᴐ

Pink Bear

When Victoria was two years old, she owned a stuffed pink bear. Whether we were going to church, or to the store, or were at home, Tori wanted the pink bear to go with her everywhere she went. This little bear had to sleep with her, sit in her booster seat in the car, go into the store with her, and play with her. With all that activity, the bear did not look new and fluffy for long, but rather dingy and matted. The appearance of the bear did not matter because "Sweetie" was a very important part of Tori's life.

As I thought about Tori and "Sweetie," the pink bear, I wondered if the Lord were such an important part of my life? Did I want Him to go with me everywhere? Did I pay that much attention to Him at all times of the day? Are there days when everything seems to be going our way, and we sail through life with no thought of our Creator and Redeemer? Am I more like that than like Daniel who "kneeled upon his knees three times a day, and prayed, and gave thanks before his God" (Daniel 6:10). Do I pray that often? Tori played with "Sweetie" much more than that each day.

We are not naturally thankful and loving, but we learn to be from God. "We love him, because he first loved us" (I John 4:19). Many times and in different circumstances we ignore God and do not give Him the attention He deserves, but He has promised, "I will never leave thee, nor forsake thee" (Hebrews 13:5). We all remember appointments, lists, friends, programs, our children, our husband, and whatever is important to us. The pink bear was important to Tori, so she did not misplace her animal or leave the bear in the store, or the car, or at home. If Jesus is important to me, I will not leave him at church or in a dusty Bible at home. I will take Him wherever I go. He is with me if I will just acknowledge Him and let Him be a big part of my life.

CRKD

Child-training

When my children were younger, I tried to train them in the way that would make the most use of the natural talents God had given them. I tried to steer them into service areas that would benefit others, not into areas of self-fulfillment. I tried to instill in them that they should be need-fillers, not glory-grabbers. Whether I have done a good job is yet to be seen, but at least I tried by teaching and example to show them what God wanted from them.

Child-training is a never-ending job, and mothers everywhere are to be commended for taking the time to train their children. Sometimes it seems like we are getting nowhere, that everything we say is going in one ear and out the other, and that we should give up and get into a more productive field, but we keep going. Then someone will come to us and compliment our children on a character area, and we wonder where they got it! Sometimes we have the experience of telling someone authoritatively what our child will eat, or where he would like to play, or what he would like to wear, only to have that same child make a liar of us by choosing something entirely different. When our children assert their independence in areas of preference, they are maturing, but when they stray from principles we have tried to impart, it is a grievous thing. Sometimes we unwittingly give our children the impression that something is important to us by our example, such as indulging in irresponsible time-wasters or doing something that is clearly wrong. When they show an inclination in that direction, we feign ignorance ("I just don't know what happened to him. I tried to teach him the right things.")

In our local newspaper was an article about middle school youngsters spending one class period a week at a place of business to learn how that business operated. One professional who volunteered to teach the students passed out index cards on the first day of class to have them list what they wanted to learn. About 95% of the students answered, "How to make money." Many of these young people were planning to make a career of playing professional basketball or baseball. In the idealism of youth, many of us may have fantasized about the same thing and had similar goals, but is making money a worthy goal of life? Is the field of entertainment, whether sports or music, the way we want our children to go? Does anyone really need millions of dollars to be happy? If so, it will be a transitory pleasure because money will be of no use to us or them after this life is over.

Please don't misunderstand me. We want to rear children who can support themselves and serve others. I know we need money to meet our basic needs, but we should train our children to fulfill a need of someone else, to perform a service, to think of others outside their own little sphere of interest, not just work for what they want in the way of material gain.

Some young people may not have as their goal making money, but of attaining greatness. Isn't that what Jesus addresses in Matthew 6:33 when He said, "But seek ye first the kingdom of God, and his righteousness; and all these things shall be added unto you" and in chapter 20 verse 26-28 when He said, " ... whosoever will be great among you, let him be your minister; and whosoever will be chief among you, let him be your servant; even as the Son of man came not to be ministered unto, but to minister, and to give his life a ransom for many." So many of us want to be ministered to, but not serve someone else. Ministering is not a lowly job, but a high calling. Ministry is exactly what we mothers are doing when we take care of our children.

A poll was once conducted in France to ascertain the greatest Frenchman who ever lived. Of course, the experts thought Napoleon would win by a landslide. One man won by an overwhelming majority, but it was not Napoleon. Louis Pasteur was voted the greatest Frenchman who ever lived. The server had won over the warrior. The one who lost his life doing research had found it.

We keep trying to train our children in the way God wants by pointing out worthy heroes and examples, teaching them to work and earn their own way, instilling Scripture in their hearts, and seeking God's will for ourselves as well as for them. Then we have to let them go.

CZ80

3

When Never is Heard a Discouraging Word . . . Well, Almost Never

ভ৪৫

All Stressed Up and No Place to Go

Some weeks are so busy, there is something to do every moment and some place to go every night. It's a busy life serving the Lord, but not boring. There will always be something to demand our attention. Do these things make us feel "up tight," "stressed," or approaching "burn out," or "meltdown," to use current terms? Do we feel like an old-fashioned nervous breakdown is in the near future? Are we all stressed up and have no place to go to use our energy constructively?

Just being busy doing what the Lord has given us to do will not cause stress, but striving in our own strength will. Also, being angry, discontented, and covetous will make us tense and stressed. We may feel like we need to slow down, take it easy, or think of our heart and blood pressure. We may just need to take a break to relax and listen to good music. We may need to learn to laugh - at ourselves or at good jokes. Laughter and music have both been shown medically to alleviate stress, tension, and pain. We may need to get back to the Word of God and prayer. "Be still and know that I am God" (Psalm 46:10).

"O.K.," you say. "I'm going to take a break and relax, but what about tomorrow when I have a deadline to meet and my relatives are coming for a week?" I'm glad you asked. Here are a few suggestions :

1. When you get dressed, put on a smile. A smile is our best accessory with whatever we wear. "A merry heart maketh a cheerful countenance" (Proverbs 15:13).
2. Learn contentment. Look around and be thankful that we have as much as we have. There are many who do not have more than the bare necessities of life. "Godliness with contentment is great gain" (I Timothy 6:6).
3. Get rid of anger. What makes you angry? Telemarketers? Whiney children? Time pressure? Confess the anger at circumstances and seek God's forgiveness. "He that is slow to wrath is of great understanding" (Proverbs 14:29). "Be ye angry, and sin not" (Ephesians 4:26).
4. Be wise. I do not feel very wise, but I know who is and I seek His wisdom. James writes, "If any of you lack wisdom, let him ask of God, that giveth to all men liberally, and upbraideth not; and it shall be given him" (James 1:5). That's a great promise. When I feel really stupid, I can go to God and He does not berate or scold me for my ignorance, He just gives me wisdom.

If we are living for a good time or in full pursuit of pleasure, we will never find it. But if we let the Lord direct our paths, we will find happiness is a by-product of our service. "By humility and the fear of the Lord are riches, and honor, and life" (Proverbs 22:4). Let's get all dressed up because we have someplace to go – to serve the Lord.

ⳍⳍ

Disasters

After Hurricane Katrina slammed the Gulf Coast and virtually wiped out New Orleans, I was sobered by the thought of the way God can bring to nothing the best laid plans of man in an instant. Many heroic rescue efforts and the quiet courage of others were documented about the survivors of the hurricane and the helpers who rushed to their assistance.

A few years ago, a major earthquake on the west coast of the magnitude of 6.9 and 15 seconds duration, brought billions of dollars of destruction and the loss of many lives. One afternoon my husband and I were in the middle of a conversation when we felt a jarring sensation and heard the rattle of a tea set on a nearby bookshelf. It was the only earthquake I have ever experienced, and that was over in a few minutes with no damage done.

Earthquakes and mighty winds are mentioned several times in the Bible. These events along with wars, unstable political situations and other tragedies are linked with the end of the age and the coming of the Lord. In Matthew 24 the disciples asked Jesus about the signs of the end time. Part of his answer is significant in the light of current events. He said, "Ye shall hear of wars and rumors of wars; see that ye be not troubled; for all these things must come to pass, but the end is not yet. For nation shall rise against nation, and kingdom against kingdom; and there shall be famines, and pestilences, and earthquakes, in various places. All these are the beginning of sorrows." Each night on the news we witness many of these catastrophes around our globe, as well as on our own continent.

Although I may not be directly affected by a hurricane, earthquake, or war, I should take heed. What I can do is to live each day with eternity's values before me. I never know when my pleasant circumstances will be shattered in a moment. At that time my relationship with Christ will matter a great deal.

It may not be a hurricane or an earthquake that turns my world upside down. I am well aware that something could happen that could wipe us out financially, or I could be told of the diagnosis of a dreaded, fatal disease, or I could hear of a crisis with one of my children. Several years ago, a friend suddenly contracted a virus that sent her to the hospital where she was in intensive care and on a respirator for several days before it was determined that she would live. Just thinking of that incident made me reevaluate my own priorities to be sure I am living for the Lord and not for my present pleasures, because that could have been me.

Should not we who are Christians make sure we have a right relationship with the Lord and with others with whom we may have conflicts? If any reading this have not put their faith and trust in the Lord Jesus Christ, now is the day of salvation.

The writer of Proverbs says, "Boast not thyself of tomorrow; for thou knowest not what a day may bring forth" (Proverbs 27:1). Any kind of disaster could happen to any one of us at any time. We are now forewarned and need to be prepared to meet this sudden misfortune with the wisdom that comes from God. With a sudden clarification of our priorities, we can trust that He will not let anything happen to us that He has not allowed and that it will bring glory to Him.

જ્ર&

Swings

"Be still, and know that I am God" (Psalm 46:10). In this day of frenetic activity when everyone seems to move at warp speed to accomplish whatever they feel merits that kind of haste, the above Bible verse seems like an anachronism. How can God expect us to be still when there is so much to do? We are living life in the "fast lane" with meetings, working, shopping, cleaning, and taking care of children and a spouse. Some of us go from dawn to way past dusk attending to urgent matters every day. How can we squeeze it all in and still retain our sanity?

These are questions we might all ask when important

appointments press us all around, but we still should have a quiet time with the Lord. The busier we are, the more we need to come apart in fellowship with God and meditate on His promises, so we will not come apart at the seams of our lives.

We have a swing in the back of our house overlooking our backyard. Occasionally after hanging out laundry or harvesting something from the garden, I will stop for a few minutes to swing before rushing into the house. The slight movement of the swing causes me to slow my pace for a few moments. I can look at the green grass, leafy trees, and blue sky, and think of how good our life really is because of how good God is. In another place where we lived, we had a hammock stretched between two trees to serve the same purpose. My mother had a swing on the side porch of her house where she could go to get away from housework for a few minutes. It may be a porch swing or a rocking chair or some other relaxing place for you, but in any case we need to pause in the middle of our hustle and bustle.

There are physical benefits of this temporary cessation of activity. Our heart rate slows and blood pressure falls. We may even become relaxed enough to doze off in the warmth of the sun beneath the rustle of the wind in the leaves or the drone of a bee on its journey.

We might borrow an idea from homemakers of yesteryear. After a hard day's work, they would "set and rest and rock a spell and count your blessings." God knows we need to relax from our stress and exertion and meet with Him. We need this quietness that the Lord can give us. "He leadeth me beside the still waters. He restoreth my soul" (Psalm 23:2, 3). To have my soul restored is what I need in this busy world. What about you? Does your soul need restoration? Take a cup of tea to your favorite chair or swing and sit a spell and count your blessings.

⊂⊃

True Love

In our modern age when so many people claim to "fall in love" (and later fall out of "love"), love has come to mean the desire to be with someone who is pretty or handsome, and whose personality makes us feel good. Is this what love really is?

We think of hearts and flowers and valentines at a certain time of year, but love extends beyond sweet words, candy, soft music, and moonlight. Love may also be expressed in practical ways as well as romantic ways. True love meets real needs. These needs may include surprising someone you love with something they love, but it may also be cleaning house for a sick friend. It may be caring for the children of a young mother while she goes to the doctor, the store, or the library. It may be sitting with the parents of middle age friends while your friends go to the doctor, the store, or library. Love will patiently endure a teen who has most of her body pierced or tattooed. Real love tolerates the irritating habits of a spouse. Real love means when I am able to squelch someone with caustic words, I don't.

Years ago when I had a new baby and several other children, we had a good-sized garden, and a lady in our church offered to can all my tomatoes that summer. That is definitely not romantic, but it was an immensely practical way to demonstrate love when the budgets for finances and time were both quite restricted.

Sometimes distance, time limitations, circumstances, and strained personal relationships tend to diminish the feeling I have for others, but I must still love and meet needs. Sometimes my love is unrecognized, unrewarded and unreturned, but I must love anyway. I must love not because of the object of my love, but because of the commandment of God when He said, "Beloved, let us love one another: for love is of God" (I John 4:7). The changes in another person will not affect my love, if my love for Him is because God is love and has loved us and has given us of His love. In other words, my love for another should be unconditional.

My security and example of true love does not come from my

children, spouse, parents, or anyone other than God himself. It is wonderful to feel secure in God's love and to say with the apostle Paul, "For I am persuaded, that neither death, nor life, nor angels, nor principalities, nor powers, nor things present, nor things to come, nor height, nor depth, nor any other creature, shall be able to separate us from the love of God, which is in Christ Jesus our Lord" (Romans 8:38, 39). I can love others who are unlovely because I know how much God loves me and what He has done to redeem me.

God has shown true love to all of us that we might pass this amazing love on to someone else who needs it just as we did. Let's show the world what real, true love is.

08&0

Time

The rapid tempo of our society reminds me of an old Swedish proverb, "The hurrieder I go, the behinder I get." We never seem to get "caught up." Is this why we are tempted to creep through stop signs or exceed the speed limit on the highway? Are we too busy to answer the telephone so we have a machine to do it for us? Is this the reason we are not more hospitable? Are we getting more done than in past years, or are we just scurrying around in a flurry of activity? Americans in general move at such a fast pace and are so aware of time, that we buy more than 200 million watches a year.

Time is a valuable, equitable, and useful commodity. We are all given the same amount of time in a day or week, yet some people seem to accomplish so much more than others. A wise Christian has said, "There is always time to do the will of God." Finding and doing the will of God for the next five minutes should keep us busy enough that we would not waste time or get into mischief. It may be that we do not like our present assignment from the Lord. Young mothers with babies that make messes or toddlers that tear things up or break things do become exasperated, but this is one of the most significant jobs in the world. Teachers may lose heart with sullen, troubled teens who are not interested in education, but they still spend time in necessary lesson preparation. A career woman may be frustrated with the emphasis on the "bottom line" or a seeming lack of trust to make responsible decisions.

We all need to slow down to "smell the flowers," avoid the physical consequences of stress, and do what is important – the will of God. May we pray with the Psalmist, "So teach us to number our days, that we may apply our hearts unto wisdom" (Psalm 90:12).

Let's make each day count by asking the Lord what He would have us to do today. Then let's work smarter, not harder, with a joyful attitude in what we are given to do.

∽∾

Be Friendly

Don't you like to be recognized in a crowd of your friends? Isn't it nice when a salesperson will call you by name as you make a purchase with a credit card? Don't people who are friendly draw others to them? I would have to answer in the affirmative to all these questions.

In our church, our song leader frequently asks the musicians to play through a stanza of a hymn while those of us present shake hands with others. One Wednesday night a lady in the front of the church had no one sitting in the immediate vicinity. Instead of standing there alone, this lady was determined to carry out the assignment. Since I had turned around to shake the hand of someone sitting behind me, I had my back to her, but I heard these words, "Somebody shake my hand." Of course several of us did just that!

One woman I know makes me feel special each time I see her. When she sees me, her eyes light up, she grabs my hand and asks how I am and what is going on with me. She is one of the friendliest people I know. Not only do I feel special, but she treats everyone she meets like that. She has many friends.

You may say, "I'm shy and can't meet people." Hey, I'm not a hand-grabbing, back-slapping extrovert either, but we do need to be friendly. Although most women will not go to church or a meeting alone, some will. Occasionally I see a lady sitting alone in church and, if possible, I will go and sit with her. It is sad to see several women sitting alone in different parts of the auditorium. Why don't we take the initiative to get involved with others? It takes a little extra effort. It takes an effort to remember a person's name that we do not know well. It takes an effort to overcome our own insecurity and make the first move. We may be so wrapped up in ourselves and our problems, we fail to be aware of others' needs. When we have an attitude of alertness to someone else's needs or interests, we may find a kindred soul or someone from which we may learn a new thing.

All of us want and need friends, but in order to have them, we must be friendly to others. Not many of us will have someone come to us and say, "I want to be your friend, and be there for you when you have a need," but we can do that for someone else. Not many people will say to you, "Meet me and shake my hand." That may be what they want, but not many people will verbalize it. In surveying a room, I may not see anyone I know, but that should not keep me from meeting someone new. Let's be a little more bold in reaching out to others. "A man who hath friends must show himself friendly" (Proverbs 18:24).

CR&O

Cashew Nuts

I like cashew nuts. Perhaps it is because years ago my mother used to buy a few for us to eat when we went to Nashville from our little town in Tennessee on shopping trips. Maybe you are like I am in picking out the cashews from a party mix or can of mixed nuts. I even turn and shake the can to be sure I haven't missed one! Recently I saw a can of cashews on sale, so I bought it. When I opened it and began to eat them, they didn't seem quite as good as when I had to diligently search for the delicious little morsels. Even cashew nuts must bow to the law of supply and demand – the demand is greater when the supply is not as abundant.

Sometimes we think we would be happy if we had more money, would be more hospitable if we had nicer dishes, or more attractive if we had more fashionable clothes, and so on. Unless we are truly needy and destitute, these things would make little difference in our attitudes. God knows what we need and has promised to supply those needs. The writer of Proverbs deals with it in this way: " … give me neither poverty nor riches; feed me with food convenient for me, lest I be full, and deny thee, and say, Who is the Lord? Or lest I be poor, and steal, and take the name of my God in vain" (Proverbs 30:8, 9).

When I am tempted to wish for a lot of things, I must stop and remember that God gives me what I need in the right amounts. How many times have I wanted a certain thing, only to discover after obtaining the desired item, that it did not bring the fulfillment I sought? Just as I searched for cashews in a can of mixed nuts, I must seek to find true joy in God's Word. When I read diligently and ask the Lord to show me what He has for me, I find rich insights that are just what I need for that day.

Let us trust that God will take care of every detail of our lives if we leave it to Him. Someone has said that God gives the best to those who leave the choice with Him, and that is certainly true.

08℘

Red Birds

One time I observed a picture in which the artist painted a dark, desolate, stormy landscape. One spot of color transformed the entire scene … it was one warm, yellow light. Another picture used much blue to show deep shadows on a late wintry afternoon which was again transformed by one spot of color … a red bird in the corner. Last week as I was on a seldom-traveled road, I spied a cardinal flitting among bushes and small trees along a fence row. Other birds may not vacate our region for warmer climes in the wintertime, but they are not as noticeable as the brightly plumed cardinal. The Richmondena Cardinalis is the scientific name for this unmistakable red bird with a black throat and yellow conical beak. When the short days and inclement weather tend to make us all succumb to varying degrees of "cabin fever," the male cardinal is a bright spot in an otherwise somewhat colorless world. What an encouragement this small crested bird can be to us! Even his color reminds us of our Lord's blood that was shed for our sins.

Can we be a red bird of encouragement to someone? Can we be a bright spot in another's life? Can we remind them that Jesus died on the cross and shed His blood for the remission of sins? Of course we can. Some friends of mine collect redbirds of all sorts to remind them of God's goodness to them in times of trouble or of the heartening influence of a true friend. In keeping with these thoughts I looked all over town once for a birthday card with a cardinal on it for a friend. (Do you realize how difficult these cards are to find?)

Let us determine to be a bright spot in someone else's life this week. We may be able to bake a cake or make chicken soup for a mother who is sick. We may be able to watch children for another mother. We may just share our home and a meal with a homesick college student. We may tuck a note of love in the lunch or under the pillow of our husband or children.

You can think of many more ways to encourage someone, just

as the red bird brightens our winter afternoons, and I hope you will. Every time I see a cardinal, I think of the dear friends who encouraged me in times of stress or toil. They lift my mood and lighten my load like the birds of winter.

CREO

Magnificent or Mediocre?

Watching the Olympics makes us appreciate the years of work and training that go into the making of a gold medal athlete. All these young people are striving for excellence that is out of the ordinary. They are willing to put forth the effort to make precise, complicated moves that appear to be effortlessly executed and go the distance in a race to obtain the applause, accolades and medals that go with winning. They will not settle for mediocrity, as only those who are the best in any given sport will even make the Olympic team. These athletes are reaching for the magnificent.

At times we see Christians who seems to have magnificent testimonies, or wonderful marriages, or who are terrific mothers, or who excel in Bible knowledge and wisdom. This may seem to be so easy for them, but so hard for us. Again, what may seem effortless really does take focused attention and hard work. Anything else is God's grace.

We read in Daniel 5:12 that an "excellent spirit" was found in "the same Daniel." The "same Daniel" was the young man of chapter 1, verse 8 who "purposed in his heart that he would not defile himself." Of all the well-favored youths in Babylon at that time, only four were given "knowledge and skill in all learning and wisdom" by God because they determined to serve Him alone. They strove to be above average.

Another example of magnificence is the Proverbs 31 woman who "excellest them all." This woman worked for excellence while doing what God gave her to do. The Lord God himself is our example of magnificence and not mediocrity. After Moses obeyed the Lord and led the children of Israel through the Red Sea on dry ground, then God protected them by "the greatness of [his] excellency" (Exodus 15:7). Everything He made or created is perfect, right, good, and excellent. "Sing unto the Lord; for he hath done excellent things" (Isaiah 12:5). "O Lord our Lord, how excellent is thy name in all the earth!" (Psalm 8:1).

We need people today who are above average; who are not run-of-the-mill, ordinary, dull, or humdrum. We need unique men and women who are inspiring and magnificent, who are willing to pursue excellence. Will you be one of those people who will "approve things that are excellent; that ye may be sincere and without offence till the day of Christ?" (Philippians 1:10). Will you strive to do the best you can like the Olympic athletes, but with God's grace, not just your own efforts? I hope you will. I don't want to be mediocre either, so I will be right there with you.

CRLO

Scraps or Treasure?

Every once in a while, I have a "free" day, relieved of some of the pressure of commitments. One day I decided to piece a square for a quilt or pillow. The truth is that I had seen a lovely pillow in a store window and thought I could make it myself at a fraction of the retail cost. I drug out my "rag bag" and found remnants of a dress that would be suitable to make a pieced quilt square. Little bitty pieces of material that others may have thrown away were cut into small triangles and squares and sewn together to form a pleasing pattern.

Quilting may not have originated in America, but resourceful pioneer women employed this craft to reuse whatever fabric they had to make warm bed covers for their families. With the advent of well-built homes equipped with good heating, quilting was no longer necessary. In recent years, however, the art of sewing and quilting has been revived and used to make decorations for the home as well as bed quilts. In any case, when little fragments of material are precisely cut into geometric shapes and reassembled in a pattern, a thing of beauty and tremendous value emerges. With batting and backing added, the quilt is made … from scraps.

I am so glad the Lord can take us from the scrap heap of humanity and make us into vessels of beauty and honor to glorify His name. Jesus can take us worthless human beings and remake us in His image. God can't use perfect people because there are none to be found. The most gifted and dedicated of us would fall far short of perfection, but it is our frailty and weakness that make His power seem so awesome. Perhaps it is greater grace to take a person that others would disregard as being of no use for anything, that brings more glory to Him when that person accepts God's saving grace. "But God hath chosen the foolish things of the world to confound the wise; and God hath chosen the weak things of the world to confound the things which are mighty; and base things of the world, and things which are despised, hath God chosen … that, according as it is written, He that glorieth, let him glory in the Lord." (I Corinthians 1:27, 28, 31). I am so glad God chose me and can use me. I can do many things, but I am not an expert in anything. If the Lord can use me in whatever capacity, I am grateful and give all praise and glory to Him.

CRBO

Fame and Success

Donald Trump, Oprah Winfrey, Jeff Gordon, Venus Williams, or anyone else whose name is readily recognizable is said to be a household word. These people are widely known because they are at the peak of their profession. Now take the names of Peter Schultz, Robert Maurer, and Donald Keck. You may be thinking, who in the world are they? Football players, rising rock stars, car racers? No. This trio led the team that produced the first optical fiber to be used successfully in commercial telecommunications. We can talk with our son in England just like he was next door because of these thin strands of glass fiber that carry tens of thousands of messages by light waves. Since Alexander Graham Bell invented the telephone in 1876 at the age of 29, we may talk to almost anyone at any time, even across the ocean via fiber optics. We seem to honor those in the entertainment industry over those who have made a more lasting contribution to our society. Fame and success are two different entities. Success may bring fame, but fame does not necessarily mean success. Dr. Bob Jones, Sr. said, "Success is finding God's will and doing it." Many people who are virtually unknown to most of us are successful in their lives because they did what God wanted them to do. Some of the most famous people are only successful for a relatively brief period of time when we think of the lasting contribution they have made to society.

Few would recognize the name of Mr. and Mrs. Moses Carver, but that couple ransomed a weak, sickly orphan baby for the price of a horse. The baby grew up to be one of the great scientists and Christians of the world, George Washington Carver. In the field of medicine, we rarely hear of anyone having polio any more, although it used to be a dreaded disease, because Dr. Jonas Salk gave us a vaccine to prevent polio. Some, but not many, would know the name of Edward Kimball. He led one of the great preachers of our country, D. L. Moody, to Christ.

Not many of us will become famous even for a brief time, but all of us can be successful in finding and doing God's will. Some of us may be called to patiently wait by a bedside of a loved one or toil at a menial job that is absolutely necessary. We may be discouraged and hurt, or used and unappreciated, but if we are doing what God wants us to do, we are successful. We must remember, "The world passeth away, and the lust of it; but he that doeth the will of God abideth forever" (I John 2:17).

Cᔕꝏ

Kindness

Today, painful and intense dislikes are easy to find, and sensational horror stories and negative news sells newspapers. It also keeps us, as a nation, tuned in to local TV channels to get the latest news about these grisly activities. Several years ago people were talking about performing random acts of kindness, and the idea caught on. It seems that some people are rediscovering the Golden Rule, and treating others the way they would like to be treated.

This concept is certainly nothing new. The Psalmist praises God for showing "thy loving kindness in the morning and thy faithfulness every night" (Psalm 92:2). This refers to God's covenant mercy that He shows us. The prophet Jeremiah tells us the Lord said, "I have loved thee with an everlasting love; therefore with loving kindness have I drawn thee" (Jeremiah 31:3). The world needs this love. I am so glad that God loved me and drew me to Himself because I might not have believed that He could love me so, and I would not have sought Him.

God in his mercy saved us "that in the ages to come he might shew the exceeding riches of his grace in his kindness toward us through Christ Jesus" (Ephesians 2:7). God is characterized by mercy and compassion and was benevolent toward us in saving us. We can also be compassionate and show kindness to others. I have really appreciated when someone has been friendly and kind to me. I should pass this kindness on as Jesus practiced and preached in the Sermon on the Mount when He said, "Let your light so shine before men, that they may see your good works, and glorify your Father which is in heaven." People need to see our kindness so they can recognize the Father's kindness.

With the harsh and bitter abuses of our modern times, we need even more to remind others there are those who care. If we deliberately set about to be kind, there will be random times when opportunities present themselves for a smile, a kind word, a helping hand, a cheerful greeting – even to people we don't know. It may be in a grocery store when we let someone with one or two items go ahead of us in a check-out line. It may be that this opportunity will come in snarled traffic as another car tries to enter a lane or intersection. There always seems to be someone to whom a kind word will lighten their load. This will go a long way toward uplifting others and making things better for all of us - especially if we give God the glory. Let's be like the Proverbs 31 woman about whom it was said, "In her tongue is the law of kindness" (31:26).

の家め

Outward Beauty

In almost every area, we women are bombarded with the message that we must be beautiful. Not many of us were born with the kind of natural beauty that is considered the most physically alluring today. Today girls can be transformed with the skillful use of make-up, hair spray and photographic equipment from an "ugly duckling" into a glamorous image. And it is mostly image. We have seen advertisements that tell us "no one can be too rich or too thin," implying that the richer and thinner a person, the happier and more desirable that person is. We can color our naturally gray hair with hair-coloring. We can buy diet plans and exercise videos to flatten our tummies, while they fatten someone else's bank account and make us feel guilty. We can also buy false nails and eyelashes to add to the illusion of glamour while expensive clothes add to the image. All of these counterfeit ideals make us feel that our outward appearance is very important to others.

In contrast to this, the Bible in no place puts a premium on beauty. These observances were only mentioned in passing about Sarai and Rebekah who were said to be "fair to look upon" (Genesis 11:11 and 26:7), Esther who was called "fair and beautiful" (Esther 2:7), Abigail who had a "beautiful countenance" (I Samuel

25:3), and Bathsheba who was "very beautiful to look upon" (II Samuel 11:2). The inner qualities of resourcefulness and courage were shown to be what made these beautiful women stand out in history. Jezebel is one who "painted her face and tired her head" (II Kings 9:30) to impress Jehu, but this, along with her wicked and deceitful ways, ended in her destruction.

We also read of the virtue of Ruth, the prayers of Hannah, the determination of Deborah, the sensitivity of Mary, the faith of Elisabeth, the availability and thoroughness of Eunice and Lois, the hospitality of Mary and Martha, and the discernment of Priscilla, but not of their physical beauty.

The world looks for beauty, brains, and brawn, but God looks on the heart (I Samuel 16:7). God is interested in inner character, not on outward appearance, and will sacrifice outward beauty to enhance inner qualities. We read in Proverbs 31:30, "Favor is deceitful, and beauty is vain: but a woman that feareth the Lord, she shall be praised."

When I was growing up, I knew a woman who was called ugly by someone who did not know her. This woman was the first to take her famous jam cake to anyone who needed food for guests or needed extra comfort. She supported her husband, her children and her church. As a child, I never thought about the way she looked, I just accepted her the way she was because she was so kind, generous and good natured toward everyone. She was a good example of the kind of person I want to be.

Most of us do not have the outward beauty the world finds so attractive. Let's not allow that to discourage us, but work on the God-given qualities that make us precious to the Lord. Outward beauty fades, but inner beauty only grows better as we let the Holy Spirit work in our lives. I am glad to know that God looks on the heart and not on outward appearance.

CS80

Dealing with Pain

Ouch! A paper cut is very painful even while it is not serious. Oh, oh, … oh, boy! I have known excruciating pain with a broken leg. At one time or another, we all experience physical pain. What really hurts even more is when I feel rejected or depressed because of a loss. In addition to physical pain, we will also have spiritual or emotional suffering. Just as physical sense receptors send messages of pain to the brain, our spiritual senses should prod us to stay in communication with God as suffering intensifies. Pain gets our attention and reminds us to be attentive to God's directives and teachings as well as to His comfort just as we pay attention to cuts and bruises.

The entire body is aware of pain in one part because of the tension it produces and loss of function of that part. Because of this, the rest of the body will come to the aid of that injured member to reduce or eliminate the infirmity. The first line of defense for injury is the blood stream. Platelets seal off a wound while white cells gather to fight the invaders to prevent or clear infection. When a member of our church body is hurt, we should come to his assistance as soon as we are aware of the situation. Just as physical pain demands action, persecution and spiritual affliction should also enlist the support of other Christians.

At times our suffering is the result of our own foolishness or short-sightedness. If I make a wrong choice, I will live with the consequences of that choice. If I don't plan ahead I may be left with no way to meet an immediate contingency. We would all like to be indulged and protected from every harm, but we all need to learn the cause and effect relationship of our choices and actions. When our suffering leads us to seek God's comfort, we will learn much. The Psalmist says, "It is good for me that I have been afflicted; that I might learn thy statues" (Psalm 119:71). Failures in our lives may help us learn to obey God and to learn of God's goodness if we are open and alert to learn.

There may also be times when we suffer wrongfully, that is,

we suffer for doing the right thing. If I happened to be rebuked or censured for the name of Christ, I should be happy. If I suffer for being a Christian, it glorifies God. In those cases, we will be blessed with joy and strength from the Lord (I Peter 4:12-16).

The Old Testament prophet tells us that Jesus was a "man of sorrows and acquainted with grief ... he hath borne our griefs, and carried our sorrows ... he was oppressed, and he was afflicted" (Isaiah 53:3, 4, 7). Because He has been through it, Jesus is well aware of any pain we undergo and is ready to help. Our pain and suffering remind us the goal is that we "may know him, and the power of his resurrection, and the fellowship of his sufferings, being made conformable unto his death" (Philippians 3:10).

Let's not waste pain, but use it to learn to lean on Jesus and learn from Him. It will draw us closer to God and His strength and comfort as we seek His assurance and guidance through it.

CRBD

Good-byes

When our married children and their families are here with us for any amount of time, our house appears to be a disaster area, with toys strewn around and things in general disarray from having so many people, things, and small children together in a confined space. There are also peals of laughter, squeals of delight from a baby, many smiles, and fun. There are meals to be prepared, eaten and cleaned up, loads of laundry to be done, folded and put away, furniture to be straightened, toys to be picked up, and schedules to be juggled . . . but we have a ball.

After a week one family bid us adieu, then the other family expressed their farewells and left. My husband went to work, and I was at home with memories of a delightful week with my children and grandchildren. There was a house to clean and laundry to do (again), but it was so quiet . . . too quiet. A silent house may stay clean, but it is no fun. Everything may be dusted and in place, but it does not bring the joy of romping with a toddler or holding a baby.

Good-byes are always sad to me because it means leaving loved ones for awhile. We will not be together to laugh, cry, hug, talk, or see each other. I like that old song, "We'll Never Say Good-bye In Glory." We will never even have to say "Good night" in heaven because there will be no night. "The glory of God did lighten it, and the Lamb is the light thereof" (Revelation 21:23). We will forever be with Jesus and with those who are in Christ. We will enjoy the marriage supper of the Lamb and the joys of heaven for all eternity. If those in our family are saved, we will say "Good-bye," but it will only be temporary. We will forever be together in heaven where there are no "Good-byes." That is a great comfort, but we need to get busy to make sure all in the family and our friends know Jesus Christ as a personal Savior.

Let's win others that we may have the satisfaction of knowing someday we will never have to be separated by time or distance, and we will never have to say "Good-bye" again.

⊂ॐ৲

4

Mary, Mary . . . How Does Your Garden Grow?

∽∝

A Watered Garden

"Their soul shall be as a watered garden" (Jeremiah 31:12b).

Though the primary application of this verse refers to the restoration of Israel, we may also look at it as an analogy between a watered garden and our own soul. After a dry spell any farmer or gardener loves to see, hear, and feel a gentle, nourishing, life-giving rain for several reasons. Some farmers call this a "million dollar rain." When the ground is dry and hard, it is very difficult to cultivate crops or pull weeds that seem to be anchored in bricks. On the other hand, a watered garden is submissive to the gardener. The soil can easily be worked, and weeds yield to a gentle tug. An obedient Christian can also be like that – easily entreated, submissive to Jesus, submissive to the hand of God, a person who can say with the Psalmist, "I delight to do thy will, O God" (Psalm 40:8).

Sometimes the rains do not come, and we must water our plants and gardens. Water is essential to all plants, but in varying degrees. Too little water is deadly to some plants, while too much is bad for others. We must know our crops and their needs. We must know the needs of our children or those with whom we work. Some will be turned off by too much quoting of the Bible, while others absorb every word. We should use discretion in speaking of holy things.

A watered garden has great potential. There are minerals in the rich, fertile soil that are transmitted to the growing plants. We must have a teachable spirit. If we are stubborn, there is much we will miss that needs to be transferred to us by mentors and circumstances. If we are teachable, we will grow in grace and wisdom and be able to discern new insights from the Word of God.

A watered garden is productive. An abundance of beans, cantaloupes, tomatoes, broccoli, peppers, cucumbers, and other vegetables as well as flowers may be harvested from a good garden. A wise Christian will be productive and win all kinds of souls - children, mothers, fathers, brothers, and those from different races, nationalities, and personalities. "He that winneth souls is wise" (Proverbs 11:30).

As you tend your gardens (even if you must water them), ask yourself if you are submissive to the "Gardener," the Lord Jesus Christ, if you have a teachable spirit, and if you are productive.

"And the Lord shall guide thee continually, and satisfy thy soul in drought, and make fat thy bones: and thou shalt be like a watered garden, and like a spring of water, whose waters fail not" (Isaiah 58:11). This verse is God's promise to Christians who fast, pray, give, and serve. Our souls reap the harvest of these activities just like a garden that receives sufficient water. Let's look at some of these benefits.

On a quiet summer night in the South we can sit back and almost see tomatoes filling with juice, ripening and begging to be caught before their tenuous hold on the vine finally gives way. In the Midwest we can "hear" the corn grow in July. This is such a peaceful feeling. God gives us peace that the world cannot understand, nor indeed know. God-given peace is a settled calmness in the midst of adverse circumstances. When we stop worrying and start praying about everything with thanksgiving, then the peace of God, which passes all understanding shall keep or garrison our hearts and minds (Philippians 4:6, 7).

A watered garden satisfies the needs of others. A watered garden produces food for strengthening the body and flowers produce delight for the soul. A garden also produces weeds, but a wise gardener will be faithful with hoe or hand to dig or pull weeds. We may have to go through disappointments or a crisis to get rid of sin in our life, and it will feel like weeds are being torn out of our hearts. We all must go through suffering before we are able to minister to the needs of others, but we will be a blessing to them. We can take prepared food to those just home from the hospital, or who are bereaved. We can be hospitable and provide shelter to others. We can offer spiritual refreshment and support of still more people. Loneliness stalks every neighborhood, and many do not want to ask for help for basic requirements. We must pray that God will make us more sensitive to those in need and enable us to meet these needs. "Bear ye one another's burdens, and so fulfil the law of Christ" (Galatians 6:2).

I hope your soul is like a watered garden - peaceful, obedient, and productive, as well as a beautiful place where friends and neighbors will be drawn in to learn of the love of God.

 CRWO

Bloom Where You Are

Driving on almost any road in the summer, with the exception of a major urban thoroughfare or a super highway, you will be able to see wildflowers in abundance. On some major expressways there are flowers someone has planted to make our commute or travel more pleasant. However, no one has planted or cultivated the cornflowers or sweet peas that grow beside country lanes, and often they are unnoticed or cut down. Still they grow and bloom, though "Solomon in all his glory was not arrayed like one of these" (Matthew 6:29). Most wildflowers grow vigorously in adverse conditions. They are also adaptable and tolerant. I wish flowers I plant in my yard were as hardy as the wildflowers I see in the woods or along roadsides.

All these pretty flowers do is bloom where they are. That is what they are designed to do. Do I fulfill that for which I was created like one of these wildflowers? Do I bloom where I am in spite of circumstances and being unappreciated? Do I brighten someone else's day by doing what God wants me to, glorifying Him? Or do I wilt and droop and make others feel uncomfortable while hearing my laments and seeing my depressed countenance?

If I am tempted to worry about my lot in life, I need only to look back to Matthew 6 to see that just as God provides for the fowls of the air and clothes the lilies of the field, He will take care of me as I seek Him first. There's the catch. I want to seek my own will, to do what I perceive as best for me. When I finally get through my head that I need to seek God and His glory, I find that He will make sure I am clothed and fed. At that point, I will be satisfied with what the Lord gives me to do and not look at what someone else is doing. Then I will "brighten the corner" wherever I am just like the lovely wildflowers that God planted.

Are you a blessing where you are planted? It may not be what you wanted, but you can seek God and His will wherever you are. Wherever you find yourself today, bloom and brighten your own corner of the world just like the wildflowers.

CB8O

Corn

There are not many treats better than fresh corn in the summertime. The succulent, yellow or white kernels are so sweet and good as I bite into them that the flavor is just yummy. Fresh corn is so much better than store-bought corn that it seems almost a different vegetable. For those who are too busy eating to notice, there is always an even number of rows on the cob.

There are numerous kernels of corn (25 to 45 depending on the length of the ear) on each row, and there are usually at least three ears of corn on each stalk. Do you realize that each stalk of corn with its three ears and well over 1,000 individual kernels comes from one small kernel or "seed" of corn? Isn't that amazing?

When a farmer or gardener plants corn, he or she knows that each seed that grows will produce much more than itself. We have just demonstrated the multiplication of corn from one "seed" to over 1,000 new seeds. The more seeds sown, the more vegetables grown. Out of every few seeds sown, some will not germinate, some will be taken away by birds or other creatures, and some may rot, but many will grow and produce an abundant harvest.

We read in II Corinthians 9:6, "He which soweth sparingly shall reap also sparingly; and he which soweth bountifully shall reap also bountifully." Although we have been looking at sowing corn or other vegetables, the context of this verse is about giving. Look at the next two verses. "Every man according as he purposeth in his heart, so let him give; not grudgingly, or of necessity: for God loveth a cheerful giver. And God is able to make all grace abound toward you; that ye always having all sufficiency in all things may abound to every good work." According to these verses, we need not only to sow much seed to reap a bountiful harvest of vegetables, but we also need to give to the need of others that we may reap a bountiful harvest of blessings. These blessings are many times spiritual, but many times they are also physical. God will see that we have all we need as we minister to others.

Remember the harvest in God's world as you bite into those juicy kernels of corn. Let's enjoy the harvest of wholesome foods from our gardens, but remember to give to others in need just as we sow much seed. "And let us not be weary in well doing, for in due season we shall reap, if we faint not" (Galatians 6:9).

Roses

I love roses - their fragrance, color, and velvety soft texture. Roses are an elegant flower signifying love. No other flower has charmed our imagination in literature and art like the rose. Roses are expensive because there is much labor required to bring forth the bloom at the right time. They must be fertilized, cultivated, pruned, sprayed, and mulched. After cutting roses, they must be kept cool and put in water or they will wilt in minutes. Even under the best of circumstances, roses only last a few days at most. Other hardier flowers require much less care to grow and display and last longer after being cut. Why, then, do so many people grow and give roses? We feel like they are worth it. When we are presented with anything so beautiful and expensive, it makes us feel cherished.

Have you ever thought God also feels our love when we offer something precious to Him? Even though God is omnipotent, omniscient and loved us first, He still wants to know of our love. David gave God such a gift when he poured out the water from the well of Bethlehem that three men had endangered their lives to get. In the cave of Adullam, David longed for the water. When his good friends fetched the water without regard to potential loss or injury, David "would not drink of it, but poured it out to the Lord." The water was precious because of the great risk involved to obtain it (I Chronicles 11:15-19).

What can we give to God to show our love for Him? It may be to give our sons to preach the gospel of Christ. We can give our time and money in travel to help a missionary, to give out gospel tracts, in a visit to a lonely person, or in preparation of a meal. We can give our possessions to someone who needs them more than we do. We can give ourselves to be used in whatever way the Lord chooses, a life of obedience and praise.

Just like the time and effort required to bring forth beautiful roses, whatever we spend time and effort on is what is valuable to us. That is what we can give to God - a sacrifice from our life.

Just like the woman who broke the alabaster box, we should give whatever we give lavishly. God deserves the best. The ointment from the alabaster box was costly. It is not sacrifice if we give the Lord what costs us nothing. We should give to show our love to our Savior who gave His life for us. Just as we enjoy the symmetry and color of a rose, I think God enjoys seeing us as we serve and praise Him. Let's give God the best that we have and are.

CℨℰⱲ

A Rose

One of the most regal flowers that has captured the affection of so many for centuries is the rose. Native to the North Temperate Zone and even southward to the mountains of Mexico, a rose is a hardy shrub of the genus Rosa that is the national flower of England, and the state flower of New York, North Dakota and Iowa. Roses have been celebrated, romanticized, domesticated, cultivated, and hybridized to give us the many varieties available today. A breathtaking scene is a formal rose garden, although roses may be grown in informal flower gardens as well as edging a walkway or driveway. Milton described paradise as having "flowers of all hue, and without thorn the rose." Loved by all, the rose is called the Queen of Flowers and is the symbol of friendship.

What is it about this stately flower that has inspired artist, poet, singer, and orator to try to describe its loveliness, though its natural beauty cannot be captured on paper, canvas, or note? Horticulturalists and gardeners spend hours working with a rose bush to produce the noble and dignified blooms. We are awed at the delicate symmetry of the handiwork of the Creator of the earth, the Lord God. And yet, a rose is mentioned only twice in the Bible in Isaiah 35:1, "the desert shall blossom as a rose," and Song of Solomon 2:1, "I am the rose of Sharon." In these verses the rose is not the hybrid tea rose we are accustomed to.

Any of us may plant, water, mulch, fertilize, spray, and coax a rose bush to produce its flower, but only God can make a rose. God in his kindness toward us gave us richly all things to enjoy, including the rose. The rose adorns the cottage of the poor as well as the mansion of the rich. It is found in the ghetto as well as the garden of the White House, and is cut by the hands of the saint as well as the sinner. A rose brightens any container - a magnificent cut glass bowl or a humble pickle jar. A rose can melt a lover's heart, comfort a broken heart, and cheer a grieving heart.

To see, touch, and smell a magnificent rose is a sensual experience that reminds us of the creativity and caring of our Creator. Of velvety texture and heady fragrance in a multiplicity of colors, the rose is truly a lovely gift. Let's thank our great and gracious God for giving us the rose.

ය‍ණ

5

One Nation Under God ...

 C3&O

Fireworks and Picnics

On the Fourth of July, the day we celebrate our independence from England, we hear patriotic songs. Every time we sing the "Star Spangled Banner." I am fine through the first part of the anthem, but when we come to the words, "O say does that star-spangled banner yet wave, o'er the land of the free and the home of the brave," a lump swells in my throat so I cannot sing. A patriotic feeling wells up in me that makes me teary-eyed to think of those who fought and died through the years, that we might be free today to worship however we want . . . or not worship anything if we wish. In our free country, there are many things about which we may disagree, but we can do so and not be arrested.

This year we can bite into a juicy hamburger or hot dog right off the grill and savor the flavor. Don't potato salad and baked beans taste even better on the Fourth? Isn't that slice of watermelon sweeter on our national holiday? Even the ants and flies are an expected part of the festivities. If you are not into picnics, you could go to McDonald's, Dairy Queen or Taco Bell; it's your choice. Our children can play in the yard until dark, then enjoy fireworks bursting in the air instead of bombs falling on their homes. We can display the flag and decorate the patio or home in colors of red, white and blue in honor of our great country.

From the Empire State to the Golden Gate, from the Upper Peninsula of Michigan to Key West, we are one union and can celebrate our unity and liberty. What a great country! I can sing "My country, 'tis of Thee, sweet land of liberty ..." because it is of God's grace we are free. Take the day off from work to get together with family and friends, but remember to worship in the house of the Lord because we are still "one nation, under God," at least for now. "Happy is that people whose God is the Lord" (Psalm 144:15).

ৎ৪৹

I Love America

I love America. I love the rolling hills of Tennessee, the picturesque Blue Ridge, the Midwestern corn fields, prairies with amber waves of grain, and the desert Southwest. In our great nation we also have ethnic as well as geographical diversity. I'm thankful for the Chinese classes held in our church building. I'm glad to know some of the Hispanic and Black community and be able to minister to them. Even with all the different cultures represented in our land, we are one nation, free to live and work and worship in the way we choose. I'm thankful for the godly wisdom of the founders of our country in the way they framed that great document, the United States Constitution.

One week a major supermarket in our area closed, then opened three days later in another location. In the process of moving, the workers had taken much of the inventory to the new store, leaving mostly empty shelves in the old one. When I saw the empty shelves, it reminded me of how much we take our abundance for granted while those in other countries often lack basic necessities. Even though we have various domestic problems, we are free from the religious and economic repression that those in other places experience.

When we celebrate the Fourth of July holiday - as we play at leisure time activities, watch parades and fly the flag, let's remember the freedoms and prosperity we do have in our republic. When we attend the church of our choice, let's thank God we can worship when and where we please. At a well-stocked supermarket, let's be thankful we have so many of each item from which to choose, that the shelves are not empty. Let's pray for those in other lands who do not enjoy these benefits and praise God for His blessings to us. "Blessed is the nation whose God is the Lord" (Psalm 33:12).

⊗

Freedoms

A few years ago my husband and I and another couple were traveling through the vast country of China. From Beijing to Xian to Xining we saw much of the cities and countryside for two weeks by air, rail, and car. In every city our passport information was carefully copied for the authorities. Even staying in the home of friends, we had to register with the government. And they checked our registration! I know, because I had written an incorrect date, and someone called to question it and straighten it out. We were also photographed in another area.

How would you like it if you had to report to some government office every time you went to visit relatives in another state or entertained visitors from another country? We would not like those restraints and restrictions. We take our freedoms for granted here because we've always enjoyed the liberty under which we live in America.

Our missionaries in foreign lands must always be careful to watch what they say and to whom. They are doing a tremendous job, but in some countries they may suffer for not being circumspect. Other nations do not have a Constitution like ours to guarantee our freedoms.

Our laws are not perfect and our nation is not everything we want it to be, but we can live here according to God's laws if we so choose. We can endeavor to do God's will "in the midst of a perverse nation, among whom ye shine as lights in the world; holding forth the word of life; ... " (Philippians 2:15, 16). Let's pause on each Independence Day and every day throughout the year to remember that we do live in the "land of the free and the home of the brave" because of God's grace. Let's thank God for America, and not take this liberty for granted.

Let's also exercise our right to vote in this great republic. Many people think "My one vote won't count," but it does. Every vote counts, but if you don't vote, don't complain about who is elected. We are all so busy trying to "get ahead" or just keep up, we do not feel we have the time to get to know the candidates or search the issues. Whether the person we think best for the job is elected or not, we still have a responsibility to respect our leaders because of the position they hold. Let's pray for wisdom before voting and pray afterward for whomever is elected, but let's vote! The Bible says "Righteousness exalteth a nation" (Proverbs 14:34). Let's vote for the ones who will keep righteousness before us. This is one thing we can do to "promote the general welfare" of our nation as mentioned in the Preamble of our Constitution and to ensure we will not live under a government without the guiding principles we now enjoy.

CRO

God Bless America

In 1888 a baby boy was born in Temin, Russia, and named Israel Baline. At the age of four, the boy was brought to New York City where he grew up on the Lower East Side. After a succession of jobs following his father's early death, he began to write his own music, many of which became well-known songs. You may be familiar with such songs as "Blue Skies,"

"Easter Parade," and "White Christmas." Changing his name to Irving Berlin, he published over 750 songs. While serving in World War I, Berlin wrote army songs. Years later he raised over nine million dollars for the Army and Navy Relief Fund in World War II.

Among the most famous of Berlin's songs with continuing popularity is "God Bless America." This prayer for the blessing of the Almighty is not found in our hymn books, although it is known by almost all Americans. Whether you remember Kate Smith belting out the tune, or just know the melody and words, it ranks with our most patriotic songs in stirring our hearts.

Yes, we do want God to "bless America, land that we love," just as that young Russian immigrant did. We want Him to "stand beside us and guide us through the night with the light from above." But let's stop and think. Can we really ask God to bless us when we have drifted so far from the ideal of our founding fathers? We read in Psalm 33:12, "Blessed is the nation whose God is the Lord." Is the Creator God our Lord or is the dollar our God? Do we put God first in our lives or ourselves first? When the economy is good and there is no war to threaten us or our interests, we easily slip into complacency.

We do love our land, and we do want God to bless our country, but we also have a responsibility to live "soberly, righteously and godly in this present world" (Titus 2:12).

 below

Independence Day

July, to most of the citizens of the United States of America, means picnics, warm weather, vacations, family, flags, and independence. As we venture out of our air-conditioned buildings into the warm sunlight and blue skies, many of us will savor biting into a juicy hamburger or hot dog slathered with mustard or catsup, or barbecued chicken and potato salad, accompanied by crisp chips and icy soft drinks. Young people will play softball, soccer, or volleyball, and listen teary-eyed to our national anthem, as well as the toe-tapping rhythms of our patriotic marches. On July 4th we collectively celebrate our independence as a free nation founded on godly principles.

But, I'm sad because many of the values of the past are being shed by some in favor of "new" values based on feelings and other mercurial, pragmatic views. Many have rejected the notion that we were made by God and are accountable to Him, and that He established a moral order to the universe. I'm sad because in the name of free speech, some feel we have a "right" to unrestrained expression, which has degenerated to vulgar vocalization in too many cases. Too many young people feel isolated, hurt, rejected, abused, angry, and anxious, and seek a pharmaceutical high to block out this trauma. I'm sad because so many of us are so hooked on materialism that hardly anyone is home anymore cooking and cleaning and nurturing children. In a large percentage of "nuclear" families, children are left with "caregivers" so two paychecks can be brought home. I realize some women really have to work and I want to be sensitive to them, not rebuking them. I'm sad because we have come through the "gay" nineties and are not better off than we were. We seem to have forgotten that "Righteousness exalteth a nation: but sin is a reproach to any people" (Proverbs 14:34).

C③හ

The Fourth of July

In mid-summer Americans all over the continent will be celebrating Independence Day by pigging out. We will grill hot dogs and hamburgers, and add to that potato salad, baked beans, Twinkies, cakes, pies, ice cream, and watermelon. While Dad dons an apron for grilling, Mom is cooking, finding beach gear, slathering sunblock on children, and worrying about how long the food will be out before food poisoning will set in, and just how many calories in a small piece of pie. Perhaps we celebrate our bounty as much as independence.

As we observe another uniquely American holiday, we should think of how we came to this point. A year after the Revolutionary War had started, Virginian Thomas Jefferson drafted a document to assert our independence from England. Congress pared down the excessive language to its succinct form, and on July 4, 1776, the Declaration of Independence was approved. On that hot summer day, those men were not thinking of a holiday. Those who signed that document were committing an act of treason against the British Crown, but signed with steady hearts.

Of the 56 who signed the Declaration of Independence, many went on to attain high political office, but many others who pledged their "lives, fortunes, and sacred honor" lost everything but their honor. Some were captured and imprisoned, some lost their lives in battle, some lost wives or children, and some had their homes attacked. The most well-known signer to us is John Hancock because his signature is so large. Hancock, with a reward in the amount of 500 English pounds on his head, wrote in bold letters to match his determination, so John Bull could read his name without spectacles. Many of these wealthy men died impoverished, so we could be free.

As we listen to stirring marches and our national anthem, as we watch fireworks and enjoy the good life, let's remember our forefathers who sacrificed so much for our independence. Let's thank God who has blessed us above other nations, not because we are the most intelligent, or most tolerant nation, but because those patriots who have gone before us looked to the Lord for His leadership in our new country and asked God's blessing in every undertaking. "Yea, happy is that people whose God is the Lord" (Psalm 144:15).

CRBO

Patriotism

Do you know the words to our national anthem? Have you ever read the Declaration of Independence? Are you thankful for the privilege of being born in a free country under a red, white, and blue flag that symbolizes that freedom? Do we remember those in the armed services today who maintain our freedom? Do we think of our fathers who fought to insure our present freedom? Have we given thanks for our ancestors who gave their lives, fortunes, and sacred honor to establish a nation under God? An affirmative answer on these questions means patriotism, a devotion to our country.

Now over two centuries later, we are still reaping the blessings of those patriots who gave so much of themselves in the founding of this country. After Thomas Jefferson, the leading draftsman, wrote the first draft of the Declaration of Independence assisted by John Adams and Benjamin Franklin, a few words were changed by the Continental Congress before it was ordered printed on July 4, 1776, so members of the Congress could have copies. John Dunlap printed the Declaration of Independence, and these prints are now called "Dunlap Broadsides." Twenty-four copies are known to exist, two of which are in the Library of Congress, and one of these was Washington's personal copy. This document gave a theory which justified political revolution and enumerated the reasons the colonists were driven to revolution. The Declaration of Independence went on to list grievances against the British government and, in particular, King George III to show that these complaints gave the people just cause in breaking away from British rule. The idea of self-rule set forth in the Declaration was the basic foundation of a democratic government.

On August 2, this famous document was signed by the president of the Continental Congress, John Hancock, of Massachusetts, along with other delegates. With no television news or telephones to spread the news of America's independence, it took as long as two months for the word to get around, so our country's first Independence Day was celebrated on many different days.

We can make history come alive as we review these long ago events and teach our children to know and respect the principles under which our country was established, and to honor our flag. However, if we pledge allegiance to our flag and forsake God's commands, we are not honoring God or our country. We must lead by example and teach our children by our instruction to be godly citizens of our nation.

Independence Day is a time to refresh our own allegiance to our great country and remember why we are able to live and celebrate this event without fear of retribution. We are not free to do as we please because we are better than people in other countries, but because of God's grace to us from the foundation of our nation. The Declaration of Independence was written by men who feared God and showed a "firm reliance on the protection of Divine Providence." Let us also fear God and rely on His protection.

 C3ED

Pearl Harbor

In 1991, we heard, read, and watched much about our national disaster at Pearl Harbor 50 years ago. The surprise attack caught us unaware of any impending danger in the idyllic setting of an island in the placid Pacific Ocean. By a series of misinterpretations and mishaps, no warning was given of that assault, and as a result, many lives were lost that day.

In 2000, my husband and I were in Hawaii and went to Pearl Harbor. After noticing the swaying palm trees and calm, tranquil harbor, we boarded a Navy-operated launch for the short shuttle to the Arizona Memorial. As soon as everyone was seated, a small woman dressed in a white Navy uniform walked to the front platform and piloted us expertly to the Memorial, which is a 184-

foot-long white structure. According to the architect, Alfred Preis, the design of it "sags in the center but stands strong and vigorous at the ends [and] expresses initial defeat and ultimate victory." The Memorial spans the mid portion of the sunken battleship. In one side section the names of those killed on the Arizona are engraved in a marble wall. The overall effect is serene, though sad.

The Arizona is the final resting place of many of the ship's 1,177 crewmen who lost their lives on December 7, 1941. In the surprise attack on that morning by the Japanese, the USS Arizona exploded, having been hit by a 1,760-pound armor-piercing bomb which slammed through the deck and ignited the ammunition magazine. In less than nine minutes she sank with her crew, a total loss. The Pacific fleet was shattered. Of 96 ships in harbor that morning, at least 18 were sunk or heavily damaged. The death count was over 2,300, with almost half the casualties aboard the Arizona.

Visitors are moved by the Memorial, which is not just a part of our nation's history, but the actual hulk of the ship beneath the structure. We were caught up in a sense of patriotism as we looked up to see the American flag proudly waving against the blue Hawaiian sky overhead.

Many of us in December are in the middle of a Christmas rush to buy and sell and get gain, or at other times, we are in a slower, idle mood, and we do not realize the enemy already has a plan of attack that will catch us in an unguarded moment. This enemy attack which can occur on Christmas morning as well as in the summer or on your birthday, can be just as devastating in another way as the attack on Pearl Harbor. The enemy, of course, is the devil who is "as a roaring lion, walking about seeking whom he may devour" (I Peter 5:8).

As Paul charged Timothy we need to be "instant in season, out of season." The word instant means to take a stand or be at a post. We must always be ready to repel the enemy attack, take a stand for righteousness, and speak the truth in love. Our training for the task is diligent study - "study to show thyself approved unto God" (II Timothy 2:15). Christians, we should heed the Marine motto, *Semper Fidelis*, and always be faithful … to God.

ೞ౩౮౨

Vote!

"I exhort therefore, that, first of all, supplications, prayers, intercessions, and giving of thanks, be made for all men; for kings, and for all that are in authority; that we may lead a quiet and peaceable life in all godliness and honesty" (I Timothy 2:1, 2).

Most people would like to lead a quiet, peaceable life. Most people would like to have a family, a job to provide for them, and to enjoy that family. In order to lead this quiet, peaceable life with our families, we must pray for those in authority, including those who govern us. We must pray for ourselves to have the wisdom and discernment to make the right decisions, and for those we elect to govern in the right way.

Every four years. we are given the privilege of voting for the chief executive officer of our nation. We have the privilege that people in some other countries do not have – expressing our opinion for the candidate of our choice for the highest public office of our land. We will not all agree, but we all have a vote to be counted. To cast an intelligent vote, we must be able to recognize the qualities that make a good president. We must ask ourselves which candidate has taken a stand on the side of scriptural principles, has the most concern for the greatest number of citizens, who will deal with moral and economic problems of our nation in a good way, and who will provide leadership for our interests abroad and at home. When we are responsible to find a candidate's stand on these and other issues, we are ready to vote.

Whatever the outcome of our election, we must remember

that we, as a nation, made the decision, and we must follow our leader. We read in Romans 13:1, "Let every soul be subject unto the higher powers. For there is no power but of God: the powers that be are ordained of God." We are subject or under the authority of our chosen leaders.

Edmund Burke said many years ago, "The only thing necessary for the triumph of evil is for good men to do nothing." No matter what the weather or inconvenience, we must go to the polls and vote. It is our responsibility as Christians and as citizens of our great country. Let's do our duty and enjoy a quiet, peaceable life.

6

Come Before His Presence with Singing

⋘⋙

A Symphony of Praise

Several years ago, my husband and I were fortunate to obtain two free tickets to a sold-out performance of Gustav Mahler's Resurrection Symphony. We enjoyed not only hearing the beautiful music of the Austrian-born conductor and composer, but seeing the musicians play their various instruments from delicate harps and violins to resounding timpani and gongs. The dynamics of the different movements of sound evoked diverse emotions. For a man who had rather go to a ball game than a symphony, it brought pleasure to my husband as well as me.

A few days later I heard a bird sing outside. It was such a cheerful song piercing a gray day just as the rain had stopped. A bird began to celebrate spring and the sunshine. Robert Shumann has well said, "Music is the perfect expression of the soul."

God has been so good to us. Our gratefulness for His blessings overflows so that we "join with all nature in manifold witness to [his] great faithfulness, mercy and love" as the songwriter Thomas O. Chisholm wrote in the hymn, "Great Is Thy Faithfulness." Forced to resign his ministry after only one year due to fragile health, Thomas Chisholm supported himself as an insurance agent. Being filled with "astonishing gratefulness" for God's faithfulness through many displays of His providing care, Chisholm wrote this hymn. Doesn't this great song make you want to praise the Lord for His faithfulness to you? It is an inspiration to me.

You may not have the privilege of seeing a live performance of a good symphony orchestra, but we can all praise God, like the little bird or Thomas Chisholm, for being our Creator, Redeemer and Provider. Even if you "can't carry a note in a bucket," all of us can make a joyful noise in our hearts to the Lord and praise Him for our many blessings. "Blessed be the Lord, who daily loadeth us with benefits, even the God of our salvation. Selah" (Psalm 68:19).

CRBO

Handel's *Messiah* . . . In Russia

One of the blessings of the Christmas season is music. Although we hear the *Messiah*, Handel's most popular oratorio, at Christmas more than any other time, it is appropriate for all seasons, since it explains the redemption of man using words entirely from the Bible. Though we have opportunity to hear this marvelous piece of music every year, people in the former Soviet Union had not had this blessing for over seventy years until the demise of communism.

In February of 1992, Kazan, a city 350 miles east of Moscow, was host to the world premier performance of the *Messiah* in the Russian language. Russian words following the Russian Bible were incorporated into the music with very little loss of rhythm. The conductor and coordinators from America sent the musical scores to Russia where aspiring opera singers learned and practiced their parts. When both groups came together for rehearsal, the Americans were pleasantly surprised at the readiness of the Russians to sing the difficult music because of their advance preparation.

Since the preaching of the gospel and Christian music had been forbidden to these precious people for seventy years, the planners were pleased to see a "sold-out" crowd the first night of the performance. However, when there was a larger crowd the second night, with many sitting in the aisles who could not get a seat, but who wanted to hear the oratorio, they were amazed. Many of the listeners were hearing the music and the gospel for the first time in their lives.

What a tribute for the faithfulness of God and of God's people! From George Frederick Handel who composed the majestic music in 1741, to those who faithfully prayed over many years for the gospel to be spread in the Russian republics, prayers were answered and dreams fulfilled those nights.

As we hear Christmas music over the radio, from CD players or over public address systems in stores, it should be a reminder to pray for all those in other parts of the world who need to hear the gospel of Christ so the Christmas season can be a real celebration of the Savior's birth. We can be thankful for the freedom we have to enjoy the blessings of Christianity and especially the music of the Christmas season.

CRBO

Music

Almost everyone at one time or another listens to music. Do you find yourself singing in the shower or humming as you go about your daily work? What songs do you sing? I heard of one man who was humming a tune as he boarded an airplane when the flight attendant asked him what it was. He replied that he was humming rock music. The attendant said it didn't sound like rock music to her, so he sang the words, "Rock of Ages, cleft for me … "

Great men and women can speak to us through the music

they wrote. When we sing or listen to the musical life message of people like Philip Bliss, Fanny Crosby, Isaac Watts, and Charles Wesley, we gain rich insights into the scriptures upon which many songs were based.

Hearing hymn histories from Dr. Al Smith was fascinating to me. I never grew tired of listening to these captivating stories from one who knew many of the songwriters personally. I think of a time not too many years ago that we were in Knoxville, Tennessee, at a convention. A large banner proclaimed the words from Psalm 113:3, "From the rising of the sun to the going down of the same the Lord's name is to be praised." A day or two into the meeting, Dr. Al Smith presented us with the song he had written after meditating on this verse, "His Name Shall Be Praised." We sing it frequently in our church.

Good music in the home is also vital to the spiritually well-rounded child. A child who hears good music will develop good tastes in music. There are three basic parts of music, just as there are three basic parts of the body. The melody, which carries the tune, appeals to the spirit, drawing us to God. If, however, the music is repetitious and tense, it will leave us unfulfilled. Harmony is an arrangement of chords in support of the melody and speaks to our soul or the psychological part of us. Rhythm is a pattern of regularly recurring accents in beats that appeal to physical drives. A concealed beat is normal and healthy in the body and music, but a throbbing beat leads to sensuality and is distracting. We can ask ourselves, do the words communicate truth? Are the words based on Christ's words and godly living or is there sensual bondage, pride, and rebellion? Those who perform and those who listen should both be uplifted by good music.

Sharing the stories behind our great hymns helps cement these truths in the minds of our children, as well. Parents, we can read and research our favorite hymns and share their histories with our children. At home, we can sing hymns and gospel songs so that our children become familiar with them from an early age.

Our family and fellowship in the church becomes sweeter when we sing together. "Let the Word of Christ dwell in you richly in all wisdom; teaching and admonishing one another in psalms and hymns and spiritual songs, singing with grace in your hearts to the Lord" (Colossians 3:16).

How many of us could sing if we had no hymn book? It is important to memorize songs and hymns as well as Scripture, and it is easy. A song helps to convey the message of God's Word with a pleasing melody or catchy tune. Learning songs and hymns is also an excellent way to teach new Christians of our faith as we praise the name of the Lord.

Music is a form of worship. Let's join together with those in our family or just ourselves and the Lord to praise the Lord in song. Psalm 95:1 says, "O come, let us sing unto the Lord: let us make a joyful noise to the rock of our salvation."

☙❧

Psalms, Hymns, and Spiritual Songs

We read in Ephesians 5:19 and Colossians 3:16 that we should speak to ourselves in "psalms and hymns and spiritual songs." In reading those passages, we might think, "I can sing songs, but hymns are too 'high brow' and psalms are old-fashioned." Not true. We sing Psalms when we sing many praise choruses, such as "I will call upon the Lord, who is worthy to be praised ... " and "I will bless the Lord at all times ... " and "As the deer panteth for the water, so my soul longeth after thee ... " and "Great is the Lord and greatly to be praised...." Yes, we do sing to ourselves in Psalms.

Hymns are songs of adoration sung in praise and adoration to God. When we sing the "Doxology," we are singing a hymn to praise God. Other hymns are "O, For a Thousand Tongues to Sing" and "Love Divine, All Loves Excelling." These are majestic musical pieces which are sung to honor God, and we should be familiar with them. Spiritual songs are songs of testimony such as "A New Name in Glory" and "Saved, Saved."

Music is such an integral part of the Christian life. It is a way to express our joy in the Lord. I always enjoy singing in church, whether we sing psalms set to music, or gospel choruses, or the old hymns. Today many churches are using choruses almost exclusively. This is great, except I do not want us to lose the old hymns. These are songs sung to the Lord himself. Most of the old hymns have fascinating stories about the writer and how they came to be written. I was reminded of this on a Sunday as we sang a hymn that may not be familiar to some.

As our congregation joined together to sing "Glorious Things of Thee are Spoken," the majestic melody carried the words to my heart. This hymn was written by John Newton, a converted slave trader and sea captain who also wrote "Amazing Grace." "Glorious Things of Thee are Spoken" is one of his finest and most joyous songs. Mr. Newton, a noted English clergyman, never stopped praising God for his "sure repose" and because "He whose word cannot be broken formed thee for His own abode." God's means of meeting the needs of mankind is through the local church where we can be involved in giving the "springs of living water" to those who are thirsting for peace and truth. We are also reminded that "Grace, which like the Lord, the Giver, never fails from age to age." That's profound, the never-failing grace of God. These words can bring joy and comfort to us. This is just one hymn among many that can touch the heart and bring joy to the soul.

All these musical pieces are part of our Christian heritage. We are told in Psalm 100:1 to "Make a joyful noise unto the Lord." Some are thinking, "That's what it would be if I sing." However, all who trust in Christ's shed blood for their salvation will want to lift their voices in praise to our great Savior. Not only do we praise the Lord for His goodness to us, but we learn doctrine by singing these great hymns and songs; singing is an excellent way to memorize Scripture. When we sing these hymns and gospel songs, we let great Christian men and women share powerful spiritual insights into the Scriptures. As we memorize these musical life messages, we will be "making melody in our hearts unto the Lord" (Ephesians 5:19). Let's not lose these inestimable hymns, but let them minister to us during the song services of our church, or at home as we hum or sing them while going about our daily tasks.

CREO

Music - the Real Thing

One summer weekend we attended a community concert presented by the Lynchburg Symphony Orchestra in the city baseball stadium. We were treated to a variety of music from patriotic, to pop, to classical. We sang along with the songs of Ol' Blue Eyes as well as singing the "Star Spangled Banner" and "Take Me Out to the Ball Game." It was a fun evening for all, thanks to a generous Lynchburg physician and his wife who sponsored the event. The spectacular fireworks at the end of the evening with the orchestra playing a spirited rendition of the "1812 Overture" topped it off. We had heard most of the melodies before on recordings and enjoyed them, but there's just something about being there, hearing the music in real time and seeing the musicians at a live performance. Seeing how the players of various instruments react to the music and their surrounding elements added to the program. As we sat in the bleachers, neither the mesh curtain behind home plate nor the rain delay could dampen the spirits of the spectators or the musicians at that event.

There's something authentic and delightful about a real Christian, too. Many people may profess Christianity, but relatively few really practice it. As James puts it, "Be ye doers of the word, and not hearers only, deceiving your own selves" (James 2:22). I see Christ in the tears of repentance in a Sunday

School student's eyes, when a friend understands the difficult time I am trying to get through, and in a stranger who offers to help when I need it. What I don't want is indifference to my hurts or joys, rebellion against God, or someone who offers pious platitudes when times are tough. A person who is not saved can recognize these differences. The real thing is perceived as the genuine article by almost everyone, and quality is appreciated by those not schooled in fine arts.

The real Christian practices the Golden Rule by dealing with everyone as she would like to be treated. If I am "stuck up" or condescending, I will give others a false impression of Christ and the Christian life. If I am real, I can make another person's soul sing when she sees I am nothing without the Lord, but a true friend with Christ in my heart (John 15:5).

I do enjoy attending concerts and listening to wonderful music played by dedicated musicians. I also think others will enjoy us as Christians if we are dedicated to our Lord and show that we are having a great time serving Him.

CRBO

Second Fiddle

Listening to our orchestra play an offertory one Sunday, I was blessed to see and hear the delightful sounds from that corner of the church. It is a joy to see the maturity that has developed in the group over the years.

Someone has said the most difficult instrument to play in the orchestra is second fiddle. This play on words refers to all of us who want to be number one, numero uno. We do not want to be in subjection to anyone or be under authority. Too often we forget the depth and beauty harmony brings to a melody. All of us are told in Romans 12:3, " ... not to think of himself more highly than he ought to think, but to think soberly, according as God hath dealt to every man the measure of faith." I have to ask myself, do

I think of myself more highly than I ought to think? Sometimes, I do. Humility is not thinking of myself as nothing, but not thinking of myself at all, a freedom from pride and arrogance.

We are all uniquely different and have differing abilities, talents, and aptitudes that God has given us so we can do what no one else can do in our life and circumstances. Many of us may aspire to sing lead, play first violin, or make the best speech, but we must bow to God's plan. The Lord may want us to sing harmony (or just make a joyful noise), play a bass instrument, or be a good listener and not a speech-maker. He may want us to stay in the background, doing the "dirty work." The Lord has a plan for each of us where we can be content and happy if we find God's will and do it.

If you think about it, second fiddle is not so bad. It is a vital part of a duet, and it is also an important part of the full and harmonious sound of an orchestra. Those who support others who may have more up-front positions are just as important as the high-profile person. Each part of an orchestra is very important, just as each person in a church is needed to round out the whole body of believers. The concertmaster of an orchestra is only as important as those who tune their instruments by him. The person who plays second fiddle in a section may be the best violinist or next to the best. Someone sitting beside the first violinist in the first chair may not be as good as the first chair second violinist. Each is indispensable. To achieve the perfect harmony that many grand pieces of music need, we must have second fiddles, as well as all the other instruments.

To have harmony in homes and churches, each must do what she is given to do whether it is to take credit or have someone else take credit for a good job. The apostle Paul said in Romans 12:6-8, " … having then gifts differing according to the grace that is given to us [we should serve] with cheerfulness." Second fiddle is really not so bad.

C38O

Teens Who Love Jesus

I really like teens, although I can understand why parents get frustrated with them. However, I know teens are immature in some ways that are annoying and they may seem hard to reach, but they are also optimistic, talented, creative, and exuberant. I like their energy and idealism. Teenagers can love Christ with a love just as real as an adult, even though they have not had as long to love Him. People have said for years that teens are "going to the dogs," meaning that teens are not respectful and responsible. Some teens are like that, but many are not.

One teenage boy wrote a song we sing today that stirs our hearts. William Ralph Featherstone was a Canadian born in 1846. Shortly after his conversion at age sixteen, he wrote the hymn, "My Jesus, I Love Thee." William sent the poem to his aunt, Mrs. E. Featherstone Wilson, in Los Angeles, who sent it to England where it appeared anonymously in The London Hymnbook in 1864. This is apparently the only hymn young Featherstone wrote, because he died in 1873, before the age of twenty-seven.

In 1869, Adoniram Judson Gordon became the pastor of the Clarendon Street Baptist Church in Boston. In compiling a hymnbook for his congregation, he discovered Featherstone's hymn in The London Hymnbook with a different tune, but did not like that melody for the words of the poem. As Dr. Gordon thought about the words penned by a teenage boy, he said "in a moment of inspiration, a beautiful new air sang itself to me." With the new music, this hymn has been included in most hymnals through the years to lift us to a dearer walk with our Savior. Dr. Gordon had a remarkable ministry in New England, but he may have touched more hearts by writing new music for the loving words by William Featherstone.

It continues to amaze me that a teenage boy in Montreal, Canada, could write such words of love and devotion about our Savior. The hymn begins with Featherstone's love for the Lord and words of assurance: "I know Thou art mine ... My Gracious

Redeemer, my Savior art Thou." Verses three and four look ahead to death and beyond to heaven as he declares, "I'll love Thee in life, I will love Thee in death, and praise Thee as long as Thou lendest me breath … In mansions of glory and endless delight, I'll ever adore Thee in heaven so bright." What powerful words from one so young!

All of this precious hymn reminds us today of Jesus' sacrifice that is ours and how much it cost our Savior. We can sing this great hymn with deep feeling as we reflect on the love of Christ this song engenders in our own hearts. I love these old hymns and the stories behind them because they are not trite expressions of a shallow faith, but of a profound relationship with the true and living God.

When you see a teen hanging around with friends or on the back row of a church pew, remember the wisdom and maturity of a teen boy in Canada who expressed his heart to his Lord in a way that affects us in a good way today.

7

Seasons of Life

⚪⚫

Dusk

In the summer after supper, when the sun has begun to set and the heat of the day has dissipated, the air grows still and quiet. Birds sing their last songs, and there's a settled feeling. One can hear the nocturnal concert of katydids and crickets. It might be a little disconcerting (no pun intended) for someone who spends most of the time in air-conditioned buildings to hear these night sounds. If there's not a ball game, a meeting or another place we must hurry off to, occasionally we have the time to sit and reflect on the day's events or more philosophical considerations. Once in awhile there is a time like this when we feel that "God's in His heaven and all's right with the world." It's that fleeting moment when we have no worries or pressures, and we are able to relax in a swing, a hammock, on the porch, or in the yard, watching the children collect fireflies or just watching the grass grow. It's a time to count our blessings, to rest from our work, to think about the direction of our life, to make plans for tomorrow or next week. It is a time to praise God for the wonders of His creation and the salvation so freely offered to us sinners.

Hearing katydids and crickets reminds me of summer nights as a child. Way back then we had no television or video games to entertain us. We played in backyards in our neighborhood, running and playing, until our mothers called us home. Our youthful exuberance led us to expend energy in the pursuits of childhood which resulted in a welcome tiredness. Then the cricket's chirp and the katydid's chorus were the sounds that lulled us to slumber. When I hear those sounds, I agree with the songwriter that "This is my Father's world, and to my listening ears, all nature sings and round me rings the music of the spheres."

When these rare times come to us, we need to take advantage of them. God speaks to us today through His Word and circumstances, but He may come to us in a quiet moment of meditation, in a still, small voice like He spoke to the Prophet of old (I Kings 19). In the hustle and bustle of our busy world, we sometimes need to slow down and listen to the still, small voice of God. Quite often today we get caught up in our busy schedules, listening to radios or CDs, or watching TV or DVDs, and we do not take time to hear nature's cadence. We tend to forget about God and worry about riots, drug addiction, wars or rumors of wars, or computer viruses. This is the time when the katydids and crickets serve as a gentle reminder that life goes on according to God's plan in spite of our chaotic world.

It may not be a quiet time after supper like I have described here, but another peaceful time at daybreak, or in a prayer closet, or even on a bed of affliction. The Lord knows where we are and what we need. We have only to listen and obey Him.

Are we too busy to listen? Is our schedule overbooked? Are we overextended? If we do make time for the Lord and stop to meditate on His Word, the world will not go into a holding pattern. None of us is indispensable. We all have certain responsibilities that must be met; there are others depending on us, but we need to take time out once in awhile. Are you listening for that still, small voice? "In quietness and confidence shall be your strength" (Isaiah 30:15).

CʒᙠꙄ

Cicadas

One morning I noticed a shrill continuous sound. Had someone left water running? Was a security alarm going off down the street? Was it a small motor? After several hours, I wondered what the noise could be. I found later that cicadas emitted the eerie song. Not only did I notice the continuous whine of the male cicadas trying to attract females, but their semi-transparent shells and dead bodies littered our walk and driveway. The red-eyed, winged insects are ugly and noisy, but relatively harmless. This particular insect needs 17 years to mature and emerge. For several weeks we heard this incessant sound until the bugs "bug off" for another seventeen years.

How could anything so small make such a big impact on us? One cicada would not be a nuisance. Even a few would not disturb us since we have other varieties of cicadas each summer. This cicada invasion reminds us ALL DAY LONG that they are here by the shrill sound.

I hope we, as Christians, are not as irritating to others as the cicadas are. However, we can be very effective if we band together. Just as the many insects make their presence known by singing continuously on the same pitch so that it gets our attention, we can make our presence known by working together. We can work within our churches to reach a collective goal.

However, we may be "pitted" against one another. Because jealousy or envy may work its way into our thinking, we may avoid a group of Christians because we don't measure up to their achievements or they do not meet our particular standards. We should all be working toward the same end – to glorify God and to love one another. Those outside the church observe us and judge the whole Christian community by one small group of people instead of taking all influences into account. One person doing something may not be noticed, but several people working together harmoniously will soon be apparent to others. "For we are laborers together with God" (I Corinthians 3:9). If we all had the same goal of making Christ known, what an impact we could have in our town and community!

One time when we were building an addition to our church building, workmen observed the women who came and went at the church. From their modest, but fashionable appearance the men gained a good impression of our church. We were thrilled to hear that. No words had been exchanged, no witness overtly given, but the Lord was magnified. When we all work together we can have a tremendous impact on shaping the thrust of our community and region.

Let's try to work together to accomplish much for the Lord, and not be just a relatively harmless nuisance like the cicadas.

ය෴

Keep Your Cool!!

In August, it's hot and humid! This combination makes us quite uncomfortable. What can we do to stay cool besides avoiding strenuous exercise in the middle of the day, drink plenty of liquids, and stay in air-conditioned places? After driving two hours to a wedding one summer in a church with no air-conditioning, we were hot and tired before the ceremony began. At that time I needed to know how to keep my cool when the weather was almost unbearable.

The Bible tells us what is refreshing – good news. We read in Proverbs 25:25, "As cold waters to a thirsty soul, so is good news from a far country." It may be that you have not received any good news recently. If not, you can send good news. We can write or call our parents if they live out of state, or visit with them if they live nearby and share something good with them. We can write a friend or a missionary a note of encouragement. We can tell of souls that were saved, our dynamic teen ministry, blessings from the Word of God. We could even tell of a humorous incident that happened in the last week. Again, Proverbs 11:25 says, "... he that watereth shall be watered himself." A summer rain is refreshing as the clouds and water cool down our parched landscape. And a bit of good news we send to another can also be uplifting to them and to us as summer rains refresh our landscape and bring a measure of relief from the heat.

On one hot day I called our local time and temperature number. The synthesized voice informed me of "temperature … one hundred four." That was not official, but it was close. That is hot, but not as hot as the Lake of Fire. We should thank God every day that, in His mercy, He spared us from hell, which we all deserve. That thought should make us feel considerably cooler.

Our lawns may bake in the relentless summer heat, our electric bills may soar with the extensive use of air-conditioning, but we can stay cool as we dwell in the Word of God. Let's not "lose our cool."

CR80

Indian Summer

Following the searing heat of the summer, cooler days are welcomed. After a hard freeze or "killing frost" the days warm up, and we experience Indian summer. I love Indian summer after the first frost when the days are warm, nights cool, and the leaves change color. I like the bright autumn foliage when the sun shines through at a slant, illuminating the leaves to a glowing gold. I like the invigorating crispness in the air, ripe juicy apples that crunch when we bite into them, and leaves that float down lazily as they blithely sail to a soft resting place. I really enjoy this brief spell of warm, hazy, quiet days before the winter turbulence swirls around us with rain, sleet and snow. Indian summer was mentioned as early as 1778 in the journal of Frenchman, John de Crevecour. The term may have been used by Native American Indians as their hunting season. In any case, I appreciate these warm days and cool nights.

It would be so easy to bask in the warm temperatures and forget that winter is coming, but we might not be prepared for cold weather if we did that. Just a few years ago I took for granted our freedom and security until that terrible day of September 11th. That may have been our national Indian summer before the cold facts of terrorism and war startled us into a heightened alert status. In the same way I may roll along in my Christian life until a crisis disrupts my life, or I meet a temptation from which I cannot turn aside, and I sin. I can be lulled into all kinds of lethargy and apathy if I am not careful to meet God daily through His Word.

Psalm 119:105 says, "Thy word is a lamp unto my feet, and a light unto my path." When God's Word guides me, I will not stumble because He lights the way. I will be prepared for different circumstances even if I am in a pleasant situation at the present. I can be strong because I am trusting in the Lord and not myself. I can take comfort in Psalm 91:5, 6, "Thou shalt not be afraid for the terror by night; nor for the arrow that flieth by day; nor for the pestilence that walketh in darkness; nor for the destruction that wasteth at noonday."

When we go from the warm days of Indian summer to the chilly days of fall, it seems like a ton of leaves fall on our yard, especially when we have to rake them. The shorter days bring cold nights and early morning frost, so we crank up the wood stove or turn on the heat. I have to put away short-sleeved blouses for turtle neck shirts, and my menus turn to soups and baked goods. I try to get ready for winter in this transition time. November is a good time to shift our thinking from outside projects to inside projects. Instead of gardening, I start quilting; instead of canning, I start cooking hearty meals. I prepare for the next season.

Let's enjoy today's Indian summer while preparing for tomorrow's winter. Do we really appreciate what we have now, what we enjoy here? Someone has said, "Yesterday is history, tomorrow is a mystery, today is a gift, that's why it's called the Present." Let's thank God for today and the joy we reap from it now and not worry about tomorrow or what happened yesterday.

ଔୠ

Autumn Leaves

In the autumn of the year leaves of deciduous trees change color from green to brilliant hues of red, purple, and golden yellow. During the summer chlorophyll absorbs all the light waves, except green, which it reflects so that the leaves look green, and uses it to obtain energy needed in photosynthesis. With lower temperatures, chlorophyll is manufactured less rapidly, and gradually disappears so that other colors take its place. When summers are not too dry, temperatures are cool without heavy frosts, and the weather continues sunny and clear, maximum coloration develops in foliage. Then we approach this time called "fall" in our area when the leaves fall from the trees. In the cycle of nature, the trees become bare and dormant during the winter and go through a renewing in the spring of the year, but for a while we enjoy the lovely autumnal colors of the leaves.

Although we have enjoyed the cool shade of green leaves in summer, we are now ready for the crisp display of bright color. Some leaves do not fall off and are not attractive. Sometimes we as Christians do not let go of things of earth either. Like the leaves that turn brown and dry and hang on to the trees until the last possible moment, we hang on to the world, unwilling to give up its pleasures to become beautiful in giving ourselves for others. In the next season of our life, what will anyone remember? Will they think of one who let go of "things" to help another or will they see a dried up Christian who is hanging onto something of little eternal value?

A great missionary song by Lucy R. Meyer closes with these words: "Banish our worldliness, help us to ever live with eternity's values in view."

May we keep eternity's values in view as we let go of the world and brighten the life of another fellow pilgrim. May we not be dead, dry old things that just hang on to the past, but let us enjoy the present and reach out to the future to make the best of what we have been given.

ᘏᘡᘏ

Somewhere in the World ...

In the midst of the frenzy and flurry of Christmas shopping, baking, decorating, greetings, and singing, let us not forget that somewhere in the world are other children, parents, teens, and senior citizens that have none of the privileges and resources that we enjoy at this time of year. While we withdraw from Christmas club and bank accounts to shop for "the perfect gift" and fulfill wishes of loved ones and friends, some parents who have been driven from their homes by war and famine have nothing to give their children. While we bake numerous cakes, pies, cookies, sweets, and turkey dinners with all the trimmings, some children go to bed hungry dreaming of bread, not sugar plums.

When the weather turns cold and we see a few flakes of snow which put us in a "Christmas mood," some families in the world dread winter because of lack of fuel to keep warm at all. Somewhere in the world children huddle close to their parents trying to shut out the awful sound of gunfire so they can sleep, while our children fall into slumber in their own warm beds to the tune of lullabies or Christmas carols.

When the spicy scent of baking wafts into our houses, somewhere else other families smell the acrid odor of fires burning their houses. While we string garlands of lights on our Christmas tree and wrap our purchased treasures in bright paper, on the other side of the world mothers look out on the bleak, colorless landscape of a refugee camp.

While many of us bemoan the economy this year and say we

will only give "practical" presents for Christmas, somewhere in the world there are no toys for the children, no warm clothes, no food, no hope. When we send cards reminding us of the "good tidings of great joy," many other people have no assurance of life tomorrow much less great joy anytime.

There may not be much we can do in a direct way to relieve the suffering of many people in other parts of the world, but we can alleviate the suffering of those close to us by sharing what we have with our loved ones, friends, neighbors, and those in need. We can pray for that father whose family is scattered to hear the gospel and share it with his own children. We can pray for provision for those who are starving, homeless, and hopeless and give if we are able. We can remind ourselves and our own children of the real meaning of Christmas and not get caught up in the busyness of the season.

"Inasmuch as ye have done it unto one of the least of these my brethren, ye have done it unto me" (Matthew 25:40).

ᏬᎸᎣ

Treasures of the Snow

One winter we were inconvenienced by being snowbound for a day or two, or for as some called it, "the storm of the century." While we could not get out to go anywhere (as if there were anywhere to go with so many places closed) without a major effort of shoveling snow and driving through piles of the white stuff, it could have been much worse. Our electricity was still on, for which we were most thankful. We had plenty of warning about the storm and time to stock up on essentials. Children and young people relished a vacation from school and a chance to play in tons of powdery snow. It was an involuntary exercise program for those of us who went out in the snow just to walk or shovel.

The Lord asked Job in Job 38:22, "Hast thou entered into the treasures of the snow?" What did He mean? What are treasures in something that causes so much havoc with our lives and is such a nuisance? Think of the color of snow. It is a pure pristine blanket that covers all the flaws in any landscape. Even the Hebrew word for snow means "white." White also describes the condition of a redeemed soul, symbolizing the highest purity. Isaiah depicts our forgiven sins this way: "Though your sins be as scarlet, they shall be as white as snow" (Isaiah 1:18). The Psalmist asks God to "Wash me, and I shall be whiter than snow" (Psalm 51:7). This whiteness and purity also characterizes Jesus. Matthew 28:3 says, "His countenance was like lightning, and his raiment white as snow." Revelation 1:14 reveals, "His head and his hairs were white like wool, as white as snow." If only used to portray Jesus and the purity He gives us, snow is a treasure as a word that indicates these perfect characteristics.

Other treasures we may find might include family time together, developing a resilience and fortitude, seeing the beauty in the snow, and learning to be thankful for the goodness of God in all circumstances. A family can draw closer together at home in prayer, reading, playing games, staying warm, and digging out. That is a treasure to be counted, too. The fresh air and the exercise of shoveling snow that helped us develop resilience and fortitude are treasures. Minerals that enrich the earth as snow falls and melts show us God's goodness. As I looked out on our winter landscape early in the morning or late in the afternoon, when the sun shown obliquely over the snow in the crisp, cold air, I saw sparkles from the snow crystals on the surface that resembled diamonds sprinkled on silk. That image is a treasure. As we thank God for each season, we will look forward to the next one to see what treasures the Lord may have for us. So you can see, there are many treasures in the snow that God sends our way.

Cℛℬᴑ

A New Year

At the end of each year my Christmas decorations are down, and my home is no longer red and green. There's a bittersweet ritual I go through just before the new year. As I undecorate and try to get back to a normal diet, I look through all the Christmas cards from our wonderful friends who have remembered us. I am thankful for several friends who had life-threatening illnesses, but have recovered a measure of health. Some cards share blessings of the past year, while others are only signed. One family hundreds of miles away added a note, "We will never forget you." Some of these friends I may never see again, but I appreciate their thinking of us. While I have the cards out, I also make note of any address changes.

Another ritual I go through is to get out my old calendar and put it alongside my new one. From the old calendar I record significant events and birthdays of relatives and friends onto the new one, so I can be reminded to send cards or gifts to those who mean so much to us. Each time I go through the old calendar, images pop into my mind of what happened that year. In addition to occasional dental appointments or meetings, I have noted funerals and births, visits and trips, weddings and anniversaries, and numerous other engagements and events that make up our life. It is all documented on my calendar, but it also shows ways God has blessed us in the past twelve months. I have written down the salvation of someone close, visits with loved ones, and lunches with friends. I make note of the first snow fall, first forsythia bloom, and the first vegetable harvested from our garden. For all this I can thank the Lord for His goodness to us.

Besides looking back at our blessings, I am grateful for another year to strive for the goals I did not reach last year. No, I don't make resolutions, but I do set goals of things I want to accomplish in the coming days and weeks. It seems to me that a resolution is a declaration of intent that often is forgotten with the onset of daily pressures and responsibilities, while a goal is a target to aim for until we hit it or decide to change it. Maybe they are the same thing, only a matter of semantics. I am just glad to have more opportunities to do more. I wonder what blessings God has in store for us this year. I am looking forward to the next few weeks and months. "Blessed be the Lord, who daily loadeth us with benefits, even the God of our salvation" (Psalm 68:19).

C33O

Ground Hog's Day

On the second day of our second month the sun always seems to shine for at least a few minutes, and Old Punxsutawney Phil always seems to see his little ground hog shadow. In any case, we usually have more winter weather. In February, precipitation is sometimes in the form of freezing rain, and we are burning more wood in our wood stove trying to keep warm. One morning the sun shining through the trees transformed our ordinary, blah winter landscape into a crystalline wonderland. A few days later our "falling weather," as it is called in Virginia, was snow. My children loved it more than I. Before all of the snow was on the ground, they were out with shovels clearing the driveway and sidewalk. Their reward for this was to spend the rest of the day outside sledding, and making snow forts. For me that meant soggy or lost mittens, snow pants, hats, and water puddles everywhere. I don't stay out as much as the children because there are domestic chores that must be done, so I peer out each window as I move through the house.

As the soft, white blanket of snow fell gently on the hard, bare ground, it changed the whole effect of the outdoor scene. A flawless environment greeted us that morning before anyone had walked through the yard, or shoveled or driven through the snow. It must be this pristine beauty that caused God to use snow as a symbol of purity. He said in Isaiah 1:18, "Though your sins be as scarlet, they shall be as white as snow." King David's confession in Psalm 51, verse 7 declares, " ... wash me, and I shall be whiter than snow." The clean, white new-fallen snow shows us how God's grace can cover the dirtiest sins.

Perhaps this was the inspiration for a clerk in a post office in Philadelphia to write a poem we sing frequently entitled, "Whiter than Snow." James Nicholson was active in his church as well as being a postal clerk for his entire life. First published in 1872, this hymn was popularized by its inclusion in a book of hymns published by Ira Sankey and Philip B. Bliss. The words and tune are familiar to most of us, but do we think of what we sing? I also want the Lord Jesus to "break down every idol and cast out every foe" so He can "wash me and I shall be whiter than snow." I want Him to "help me make a complete sacrifice."

As you look at the snow or play in it or shovel it, ask the Lord to cleanse you and make you whiter than snow. This is what love and forgiveness do for us. Just as we feel cozy and protected in a warm house with snow outside, we feel warm and sheltered in the love of God. Let's thank God for His grace to us as much as to a postal clerk who wrote this lovely hymn.

CRBO

Dogwoods

"For, lo, the winter is past, the rain is over and gone; the flowers appear on the earth; the time of the singing of birds is come, and the voice of the turtle is heard in our land; ... " (Song of Solomon 2:11).

As the warm days of spring give impetus to the trees, bulbs and seeds to send out new buds and shoots, the flowering of the dogwood is a welcome sight. Soon after the redbud puts a delicate splash of color in the woods, dogwoods open their quartet of pink or white petals. Whether dogwoods grow among the taller trees of the forest, on the beautifully appointed lawn of a mansion, or beside a tarpaper shack, these small trees enhance any landscape and let us know that spring is really here.

Dogwoods are a proclamation of spring, and we should be proclaimers of the resurrection wherever we find ourselves. We do not have to dress in the latest designer fashions to witness for Christ, nor do we have to look dowdy. We do not have to live in a "good house in a nice neighborhood" to tell of the resurrection. We do not have to be married to a man who pulls in a six-figure salary to tell others of what Jesus has done for us. We can bloom where we are planted.

Everyone needs to hear the good news of salvation and its benefits. All are searching for peace which the world cannot give, and we who have this peace know it is in the person of Jesus Christ. Jesus gave this promise to His disciples and to us in John 14:27: "Peace I leave with you, my peace I give unto you: not as the world giveth, give I unto you. Let not your heart be troubled, neither let it be afraid." There are many things to trouble us in this age, but the peace that Jesus gives will transcend all of that. We can be like the serene dogwoods living in splendor in the woods. Other trees may be taller, but not more pleasing.

Too often we Christians are just like anyone else. Our neighbors can see no difference in us and in someone who does not know Christ. I must be careful that I do not just talk about the shallow, inane things of the world that everyone else seems to think about, but that my speech is gracious and not lacking intellectual or spiritual depth. I must be careful to dress modestly, while not being distracting by being out of fashion. In other words, I need to be the kind of person that others want to know, and know why I have the peace in these troubling times that only Christ can give.

People may not act like they are looking for the answers in Christ, but they are. Just as dogwoods are a sure sign of spring, we should be a sure sign of a redeemed person to our friends and neighbors. Let's be a welcome sight to those for whom Christ died, and tell them of His glorious resurrection.

CR80

Easter

The scent of "Easter" lilies brings back memories of my childhood when our family attended sunrise services on Easter Sunday morning. I remember the stained glass windows with sunlight filtering through and the glorious songs of resurrection. This was followed by a country breakfast of pancakes or biscuits, country ham and eggs with our neighbors. When we were stuffed with all that good food, we went to the morning church service. It was a special time for all of us, as it should be.

When we think about Easter, for many people this means a change of scenery or clothing, especially for us in the temperate zones. Therefore, for most people Easter is a celebration that has little or nothing to do with the resurrection of Jesus Christ. To some, Easter represents the end of the Lenten season and doing without favorite foods and festivities. To others, this time means buying new clothes to show off to friends. Easter is more than just a new dress or hairdo or washing windows and hanging new curtains. Easter Sunday is a special time to meditate on the kindness and grace of God in sending His only begotten Son to die for our sins and be raised for our justification. Easter is the time we celebrate our Lord's resurrection from the dead.

Stop and think a moment. How do we celebrate Easter? What impact has the resurrection made on our lives? In writing this, I am thinking of the empty tomb we saw in a garden just outside the city of Jerusalem. A sign on the wall proclaims what we believe and is a direct quote from Matthew 28:6. It says, "He is not here; for he is risen." This is the meaning of Easter. We do set aside a time to sing anthems of praise to God and tell others that He is risen indeed, but Easter Sunday doesn't have to be the only time to do this. Every day we should praise God for all He has done for us, for every blessing that encourages us, for every trial that makes us stronger, for every sorrow that makes us more tolerant, for every grief that draws us closer to Him and makes us sweeter. Everything that comes into my life is a benefit, and I only have to seek the lesson that God has for me through it. Each new day is an opportunity to live for Jesus and do good in His name because His mercy and compassion are new for each day.

"This is the day which the Lord hath made; we will rejoice and be glad in it" (Psalm 118:24). We should be thankful for all the days from Creation to the present. We should be thankful for the day Christ died on Calvary, for the time three days later when He arose from the grave, and the day of His ascension to heaven where is He is now interceding for us. We should be thankful for this day the Lord has given us to proclaim His glory and grace. Let's make every day, as well as the next Easter Sunday, a special one as we count our multitude of blessings.

೦೪೮೦

Easter Rabbits or The Resurrection?

"Here comes Peter Cottontail, hopping down … " But wait! What do rabbits have to do with Easter? It's tradition! Bunnies hide eggs for children to find (although rabbits produce bunnies, not eggs). An egg hunt is fun, and I've seen stories about eggs with a spiritual message. Which brings us back to rabbits. Cute, fuzzy Easter bunnies are a great sale item for merchants, but I cannot make the connection with the real reason for Easter. In some families, Easter is a cultural event marked by egg hunts and Easter baskets full of all sorts of candy and toys. College students look forward to a break from tedious studies and enjoy a vacation from school for a week. Christians may also get caught up in the traditions and miss the real meaning of the day.

The real reason for Easter is the celebration of Christ's resurrection from the dead. Jesus Christ gained the victory over death and the grave. If this life is all we have, we will be miserable with no hope. As the apostle Paul says in I Corinthians 15:17, 19, 22, " … if Christ be not raised, your faith is vain; ye are yet in your sins … If in this life only we have hope in Christ, we are of all men most miserable ... for as in Adam all die, even so in Christ shall all be made alive." The good news of the gospel is "that Christ died for our sins according to the Scriptures; and that he was buried, and that he rose again the third day according to the Scriptures" (I Corinthians 15:3, 4). That is the "gospel" truth. This is the wonder of Easter – that Christ died and rose for our justification, and that we may also rise again from the dead one day. That is a lot to look forward to. Because of this fact, we can be "steadfast, unmovable, always abounding in the work of the Lord, forasmuch as ye know that your labor is not in vain in the Lord" (I Corinthians 15:58). This is our hope.

Our hope is not in soft rabbits, but in the living Savior. These traditions are fun for the family and provide a family time, but let's not forget the real reason for Easter. A child enjoys the cuddly bunnies, whether real or stuffed, and we can enjoy our gatherings and traditions, too. While we buy fuzzy animals for our kids, cook a feast for loved ones, and buy new clothes, let's also remember God's only begotten Son who died and rose for us. The resurrection is the major point of Christianity and the pivotal point in history. Let's celebrate Easter this year keeping in mind this absolutely invaluable principle of the resurrection without which we would have no hope in this life or the one to come.

⚜

Easter Lilies

As the winter's chill gives place to warm breezes of spring, various flowers push through the sod to remind us that after death comes resurrection. Many seeds, as well as dormant bulbs, awake to produce brightly colored blooms that adorn our landscape. However, at Easter the flower we think of as representing the season is the Easter lily. In the family Liliaceae and genus Lilium, are 84 known species, of which 73 are grown in gardens or greenhouses. The Easter lily, or L. longiflorum is a herbaceous perennial with an erect, leafy stem and funnel shaped, fragrant white flowers.

The Easter lily that is so familiar to us and is used so profusely in decorations at this time of year is not mentioned in the Bible. The lilies of the field Jesus mentioned in the Sermon on the Mount are the Anemone coronarias. In early spring the ground near the plain of Gennesaret is covered with the brilliant blossoms ranging from crimson to bright purple. The lily mentioned in Song of Solomon 5:13 is the Lilium chalcedonicum, which is a rich red.

Even though not based on Scripture, the tradition of using the stately white lily at Easter can remind us of the purity and beauty of the Savior who knew no sin, but became "sin for us, that we might be made the righteousness of God in him" (II Corinthians 5:21). Just as the beauty and fragrance attracts bees to the lily in order to carry the nectar and pollen away, the message of the cross and the resurrection attracts sinners to salvation so they might carry away the message of forgiveness to a lost world. Many may not think a cross with the connotation of death would be appealing, but it is the Savior who died to satisfy the just demands of a holy God and message the cross stands for that is the attraction. The Easter lily has come to symbolize the purity of One who could fulfill the requirement of God to be holy and righteous. The wonder of it all is that God imparts this righteousness to us from the cross. Christ is an everyday reality to those who trust in His work on the cross, not just a historical fact. Hallelujah and Hosanna.

As you see the elegant lilies in homes or churches this Easter season, think of the suffering Savior who died for each of us and lives today to offer us the abundant life in Him. Let the Easter lily also remind us of the purity and sweetness of life that is possible only through Christ.

CRRO

The Savor of Honeysuckle

In the late spring when my husband and I walk around the block, we detect the sweet scent of honeysuckle. There are other daily assaults on our senses, like the stench of fumes from cars and trucks as we try to be alert to traffic while we walk on uneven pavement or bumpy ground, or the smell of dirty clothes as I do the laundry. We may hear the loud beat of a radio in a car or someone yelling at another person. We see things we had rather not see on TV or billboards or in our neighborhoods. We taste bland vegetables or worse, the bitter taste of necessary medicine. We feel the rough edges of frayed nerves. Then the gentle odor of honeysuckle is a welcome relief.

Honeysuckle grows wild. No one around here cultivates it, it just grows and tangles around trees and brush in undeveloped lots along with blackberry bushes and other weeds. Maybe God put it there for us to enjoy without having to care for it. Do you think some things are put on this earth just for our delight? I think so. There are many things like sunsets, symmetrical sea shells, the softness of a baby's skin, a mocking bird's melodious song, as well as the different scents of honeysuckle and roses and other flowers that God has given to us to bring us joy. I think the Lord wants to give us good things like we want to give our children good things for their pleasure that will cause no harm.

In the Old Testament the word *savor* is used for the word *scent*, and often qualified by the word sweet. God also appreciates a sweet smell, or scent, or savor, just like we do when we notice the perfume of the honeysuckle. Savor refers to the sacrifice which God was pleased to accept. After the flood, Noah built an altar unto the Lord and offered burnt offerings on it. We read about this sacrifice Noah made in Genesis 8:21, "And the Lord smelled a sweet savor." This is followed by the promise to Noah never to flood the earth again and the promise of the continuation of seasons. Noah's burnt offerings were accepted by God. In the New Testament savor is used metaphorically to refer to the incense burned in a victor's triumphal procession as in II Corinthians 2:14, "Now thanks be unto God, which always causeth us to triumph in Christ, and maketh manifest the savor of his knowledge by us in every place." Paul goes on to say in this same passage, "For we are unto God a sweet savor of Christ" showing a Christian's sacrifice of obedience is pleasing to God. When we practice the Golden Rule of treating others as we would wish to be treated, we are a savor to God. This is what Paul meant in Philippians 4:18, "an odor of a sweet smell, a sacrifice acceptable, well pleasing to God."

When I inhale the sweet fragrance of the honeysuckle bouquet wafting on a slight breeze, I think of the pleasure God receives when we obey Him, whether it is a direct command or indirect, such as doing a good deed no one else knows about except the fortunate recipient. These things are a delight to the Lord just as the aromatic scent from flowers is a delight to us. Each time I smell the honeysuckle, I will think of the goodness of God.

8

Photo Albums, Pony Express and Other Random Musings

⚬⚬⚬

Photo Albums

Since I acquired a single lens reflex camera several years ago and a digital camera more recently, I have taken many pictures of family, friends, places we visit, and other interesting things. I don't wait a year to have the film developed or prints made because I love to see the pictures and be reminded of a vacation, a visit with a friend, or a birthday party. Then what? What do you do with pictures? Do you put them in a shoe box on the top shelf of the closet? We should get those pictures out. Children love to see pictures of parents when we were younger. Look at your own wedding pictures and show them to your children. Show them their baby pictures and pictures of vacations. Laugh and cry together. This is a bonding time and a time we can remember with joy. We never take pictures of the bad times. Only a professional photographer using a picture for an illustration will photograph a couple having a fight and yelling at each other. We want to remember the good times.

If there is a "shutterbug" in your family, I suspect you have had many good times, too. I know we learn valuable lessons in the sad, traumatic, and "down" times, but we are uplifted by the good times. As we share this with our families, the joyful times will increase, and there will be pictures of many more happy get-togethers.

Once in a great while I get in a mood to look at the pictures and sort them out. I write names and dates on the back of every picture as soon as I get them from the photo lab. (You may think I am super-organized. I am not. I simply have a bad memory, and too many times I have looked at a picture and wondered how old a child was then, or who was in the picture.) Anyway, when a "photo album mood" hits me, I chronologically arrange photographs, label them, put them in an album, and decorate each page appropriately. It takes almost forever because I look at each picture and relive the good times that are past.

Family members and activities are most often captured on film, but we have a large number of pictures of friends. I like to take a photograph of families that visit us and occasionally send them a picture of their family. If I do not see a person, write to them, or pray for them, I will soon forget them. These photographs of families hundreds of miles away or missionaries half-way around the world from us help me to keep them in my thoughts. We know from Proverbs 17:17 that "A friend loveth at all times." In order to love my friends I like to look at their pictures, think about them, and pray for them.

One friend whom we had not seen for a few years stopped in for a brief visit on his way through our city. As we welcomed him into our home, we asked him to sign our guest book. Next, I wanted to take a photograph to remember him. He then asked, "What's next, fingerprints?" I am not really that bad, am I?

‹⁂›

Pony Express

Most of us may feel we are too busy to write a letter when we can pick up the phone or fire off an email. I realize our time is limited and the postal service in the United States is not perfect, but it is better than other places. Our oldest son, who is living in Europe, once visited one of our missionaries and sent me a postcard from that country. When we received it, the missionary had returned home and had been here for a couple of weeks on furlough! (And we thought our mail service was bad!)

For less than 40 cents, we can send a letter anywhere in our great country. For less than a dollar, we can send a letter by air mail to a friend or missionary in another country. We joke about going back to pony express when a letter takes more than a few days to reach its destination, so let's look at that system for a minute.

With the discovery of gold in California in 1848, thousands of people moved west. Mail was sent overland, but the pony express, a private enterprise, was begun to provide faster mail service to and from the Pacific region. It ran from St. Joseph, MO to Sacramento, CA, in 1860 and 1861. William F. "Buffalo Bill" Cody was one of the first riders. This distance of 1,900 miles took 40 men riding 50 miles a day on 500 of the best horses in the West just 10 days to make the trip. The best time was 7 days and 17 hours to deliver the inaugural address of President Abraham Lincoln in 1861. Postage was $5.00 a half ounce, a tremendous sum back then and a great amount even now. Later the rate was reduced to $1.00. Light clothing and small saddles were used, and no weapons were carried to conserve weight. Mail pouches were flat and letters had to be written on thin paper. Yet, each rider was presented with a full-sized Bible when he joined the pony express. When weight was counted in ounces, a Bible weighing even a pound or less added significant weight to the load. We must conclude the entrepreneurs of the pony express considered the Word of God to be absolutely necessary to the success of the operation.

How much do we value the Word of God today? Do we have a copy readily available in the car or in our purses? Many who have several copies of the Bible in their homes seldom read them. Is the Bible part of our necessary equipment for success in whatever we do? It was necessary over 150 years ago, but many companies do not want employees to bring Bibles to work, and they are banned from schools. Yes, things have changed, but is it for the better? The Word of God is our standard and our greatest resource. It is the only way we can really know God and what He wants us to do. The question for us today is: to be successful, do we want the Word or the world?

CA80

Courtesy

In the winter of 1994, flutist James Galway interrupted a concert in which he was playing with the Nashville Symphony Orchestra to lecture to those gathered on concert etiquette. Because of distracting background noise, he told the listeners that an audience of 2,000 or more in Japan could sit through an entire concert in silence, and he asked those gathered there to cover their mouths when coughing. The Nashville Banner reported that the audience enthusiastically applauded his performance. Had no one ever told them how to behave in public or how distracting their "small noise" might be to others? Apparently not.

An announcement was made in one church that those who had to leave the service were asked not to reenter the auditorium during the pastor's message, which lasted only about 20 minutes. There may have been medical or other reasons which necessitated an exit, but to use the facilities or get a drink of water, which could have been done earlier, was no excuse to leave in the middle of a service. The noise of the prolonged folding of cellophane mint wrappers is equally distracting. Babies and young children likewise draw one's attention away from what is being said. Many adults think mannerly children are suppressed or inhibited, but the opposite of polite is rude.

Courtesy is a choice in which a person yields his preference.

We all want to be comfortable all the time, but we can endure minor discomfort for a few minutes so as not to annoy someone else. All of us can prevent distractions that would keep others from hearing a concert, or lecture, or the gospel message. Manners are not a set of Victorian rules set in stone, but a sensitivity to others' needs. Courtesy is behaving a little better than is absolutely necessary. Etiquette is a set of rules for social behavior or professional conduct. Everyone needs to know how to respond to a variety of social demands.

All this points us back to the "Golden Rule." Someone has said, "He who has the gold, makes the rules." No, not at all. What a greedy way of looking at life! The Golden Rule is what mothers used to instill in their children, and some mothers still do. Jesus gave us the Golden Rule when He said, "Therefore all things whatsoever ye would that men should do to you, do ye even so to them" (Matthew 7:12). In other words, treat others the way you would like to be treated. If most of us would do this, all of us would be more comfortable in such situations. We want to be unpretentious, yet considerate; forthright, yet kind and tactful. Let's not let courtesy, this emblem of civility, erode from our society.

CRWO

Dogs, Man's Best Friend

When we had a dog, I would come home to be greeted warmly by our family dog. His wagging tail and clear brown eyes seemed to say, "Welcome home. I'm so glad to see you again." If you have a dog or have had one, think about it a minute. They are eager to see us when we wear no make-up and wear scroungy clothes, not just when we are gussied up for a big occasion. Dogs never criticize us; they accept us as we are. It does not matter to them if we have a terrific job or no job, if we are slim or need to lose weight, if we are old or young, if we are sick or in glowing health.

If we scold our pet canines, they hang their heads and slink off, but are back later, licking our hands with a silent apology. Roger Caras, a reporter on pets and wildlife, said, "We give them the love we can spare, the time we can spare. In return dogs have given us their absolute all. It is without a doubt the best deal man has ever made." Perhaps that is why dogs are known as man's best friend.

We as Christians can gain some lessons in loyalty from our family pets. Not only with our families, but also with our fellow believers, we should extend a cordial greeting when we see them. I know one woman who is the friendliest person I have ever met. She greets everyone as if she were a long-lost, but beloved friend. As a result, she has many friends. We should accept a person as he is, not as we wish he could be. Too often we have an unrealistic expectation of another and do not accept differences we all have. We should not demand time and attention, but give it and take what we may get in return. We should be content to serve if there is no reward or appreciation, although it is difficult not to want others to conform to my idea of what she should do or be.

Loyalty is adjusting my schedule to meet the needs of those I am serving. Our dog is ready to go for a walk whenever I have the time. Am I ready to walk with the Lord, or am I too busy to spend a little time or a lot of time in prayer? Do I share really intimate moments with the Lord? Do I read God's Word or just a one-short-page devotional?

Loyalty knows and follows the wishes of employers, bosses, husbands, pastors, parents, and others responsible for us. Our pets know (or should know) in which rooms they are allowed or what they may and may not chew. They know our wishes and will obey for a pat on the head and a kind word. Do we really know God's will for us or do we often make our own plans and ask for God's approval afterward?

Some dogs will wait for hours, even days, for their master to rescind the command to "Stay." Some dogs wait at the end of the yard for the school bus to arrive because they are serving a young master. Loyalty stands with others in their time of need. Will we stand with a friend who has lost a job, a husband who is ill or injured, or a child who is having a hard time adjusting to a challenge, or are we "fair weather friends?"

Yes, man's best friend has much to teach us about being faithful and true to our family, friends, and the Lord. "Greater love hath no man than this, that a man lay down his life for his friends" (John 15:13).

CR&O

Preparation for a Trip

After school is out many of us will be traveling or going on a vacation. I like to visit with friends or tour a place famous for a person, architecture, or event. I have been in 20 different countries, a few several times and some on the other side of the world. Each time I prepare for a trip, the one thing I dread most is packing to go. (The second thing I do not like about a trip is the actual travel. I like to be there, but I do not relish sitting in a car or airplane all day to get to my destination!) In order to pack a suitcase, I must decide what to take. That means deciding what activities we will be involved in, what the weather is likely to be, and what colors can be coordinated so that many outfits can be made from a minimum of clothes. So many of these decisions are in the realm of speculation, which make the choices all the more difficult.

Whether you are a homebody or like to travel, there is one trip all of us will make. The preparation for this trip is being made on a daily basis. Those who have, in a point in time, put our trust in the finished work of Jesus Christ are assured of our final destination: heaven. To prepare for the trip to heaven, we will not have to think about the weather, activities, or color coordination, as this has all been planned. However, we do not know our departure time. We must always have our "bags packed" and be ready to go at any time. "Watch, therefore; for ye know not what hour your Lord doth come" (Matthew 25:42). "For yourselves know perfectly that the day of the Lord so cometh as a thief in the night" (I Thessalonians 5:2). That day will steal upon us so that we must always be poised for immediate departure.

Perhaps it is more difficult to maintain a state of readiness for the Lord's return than to plan a vacation wardrobe, but it must be done. Just as I wash clothes and fold them carefully in a suitcase, so I must be sure my spiritual garments are clean and unwrinkled. The Word of God cleanses us "with the washing of water by the word" (Ephesians 5:26). We remove wrinkles from clothes with an iron, but from our lives with confession of sin. "Wherefore, beloved, seeing that ye look for such things, be diligent that ye may be found of him in peace, without spot, and blameless" (II Peter 3:14). Our diligence will be of great benefit to us now while we await the shout, the voice of the archangel, and the trump of God, as well as when we are found blameless at the coming of the Lord.

Enjoy your travel and have a nice vacation … but don't take a vacation from God.

☾☽

Venus Fly Trap

When he was a little boy, our youngest child became fascinated with a plant called the Doinaea Muscipula or more commonly known as the Venus Fly Trap. This curious insectivorous plant has two rounded lobes with fringed bristles on the end of its leaves. When an insect touches the sensitive hairs, the leaves suddenly snap shut to trap the unsuspecting creature. Its glands then secrete a digestive fluid that dissolves the tissue of the plant's victim, which becomes food for the plant itself. We have seen flies light on the plastic pot and crawl around the base of the plant, then up on the leaves. The fly is lured by the innocent look of the vegetation and is caught off guard, then captured.

How many times are we as Christians caught off guard by Satan's devices? He makes sin look so attractive and lures us with false promises on billboards, television, or the enthusiasm of friends. Not wanting to miss anything labeled "fun," many often ignore the diabolical price tag attached to it. The horror stories that follow are the "finished product of the brewer's art," or gambler's bet, or junkie's needle.

The old adage, "to be forewarned, is to be forearmed" needs to be heeded today. God doesn't want us to wander aimlessly into the devil's snares and traps and get caught like a fly or other insect in the Venus Fly Trap, so He has told how to avoid them. If I don't put myself in a place where I will be encouraged to do wrong, I probably will not do it. I think that is what is meant by Romans 13:14, "make not provision for the flesh, to fulfill the lusts thereof." If I don't make brownies, I won't be tempted to eat too many of them. God has given us a standard and guidelines to follow, but also has alerted us to dangers along the way. All we have to do is read the label (the Bible) and do what it says. "Wherewithal shall a young man cleanse his way? By taking heed thereto according to thy word" (Psalm 119:9).

CRLF

Going Home

Spring was a good time of year to return to our home town in Tennessee. The gently rolling, green hills sported "See Rock City" signs on the tops or sides of barns along with ads for fireworks along the roadside. Like many towns that have not experienced significant declines, national chain stores have opened in new shopping centers where we remembered farms on the outskirts of town. I like to see progress and to move forward, but I am at the same time nostalgic for the "good old days." This dichotomy helps me appreciate what we had growing up in a small town, as well as the advantages available now.

It was good to go home, but "home" is not as it once was. Sometimes I think of my mother's house in Tennessee. For years we had enjoyed the side porch swing, the peaceful trees in the backyard, the Christmas tree in the living room. All those years my parent's house was an anchor for us, a place to come home that changed little. It is all different now. My mother had to sell the house and move to a retirement home in another city. Someone else owns the house and has made changes as any new owner will do. Instead of a pale yellow house trimmed in white, the house is now red with gray and purple trim. Instead of the familiar rooms, there is new wallpaper in every room with antique furnishings. The porch swing has been replaced by a small sun room with a statue in the middle of it. A great variety of plants, a brick walkway and a fountain are now where grass used to grow in the yard. It is not the same as it was when we lived there. New owners have innovative ideas. It is the same house, but not the home where I grew up.

All things change. We must move on to meet the needs of the present. Carpet wears out and furniture breaks. They must be replaced. The act of replacing something familiar transforms it for us. It is not bad, but just different. We may want to live in the past and yearn for those good times, but we must move on. We may try to go back, like I did to the house where I grew up, but it is not the same. We can't go home again to what was there years ago.

Likewise, I remember when I was saved and the ebullient feeling that accompanied it, and, though the great feeling of being washed clean from my sins has diminished, I cannot dwell on feelings. I must live today and take advantage of the opportunities it presents. I can remember the past fondly without persistently trying to make it what it once was. We can say with the apostle Paul, "forgetting those things which are behind, and reaching forth unto those things which are before, I press toward the mark for the prize of the high calling of God in Christ Jesus"

(Philippians 3:13, 14).

Someone has said you can never go home again, meaning that we can return to a geographical location, but the circumstances that made it "home" will not be the same. The house I grew up in is not the same, and the town has changed, but I can still go on while remembering the past. Let's reach forward together.

‌ℭℨℬℭ

It'll Never Be Noticed From the Back of a Galloping Horse!

Have you ever heard this quaint expression? A good friend of mine told me her mother used to tell her, "It'll never be noticed from the back of a galloping horse," when she tended to worry about little things. That has helped me, because sometimes I am a stickler for details that don't, in the final analysis, really matter.

In piecing a square for a quilt top one day, I had put together 43 triangles and squares of material to make a larger pattern. To get all those little pieces to come out to a perfect 14-inch square, I had to cut the fabric straight and seam it true. If I didn't do this precisely, the larger square may not be straight or some parts may be puckered and not lay flat. After sewing part of the pattern together, I found that one seam was about 1/16th of an inch "off." Since it didn't alter the final dimensions of the quilt top, I let it go. It was not perfect, but it would never be noticed from the back of a galloping horse! In fact it probably would not be noticed by anyone but a good quilter.

What am I saying in all this? Sometimes we waste time haggling over minor details or agonizing over choices, and let more important items go unattended. My house does not have to be flawless to be comfortable. We should all do our best in everything, but there are times when we should realize that the house is clean enough and not spend more time on that project.

As Jesus told the Pharisees in Matthew 23:23, "Woe unto you, scribes and Pharisees, hypocrites! for ye pay tithe of mint and anise and cummin, and have omitted the weightier matters of the law, judgment, mercy, and faith: these ought ye to have done and not to leave the other undone." It is far more important to make guests feel comfortable than to have an ideal house. I have seen quilts with large stitches and corners that do not fit precisely, but they are still beautiful pieces of work.

Ladies, are we wasting time worrying about things that "don't amount to a hill o' beans," as many say? Can we discipline ourselves to not spend an inordinate amount of time on trifling effects? Life is too short to worry about most of the things with which we concern ourselves. A galloping horse is gone in a flash, and the brevity of life dictates that we put our efforts into things that will count for eternity. Our main goal should be to the praise of God's glory, and all our energies should be directed toward the accomplishing of this in our lives. The Lord knows we are not perfect, but He has called us to holiness, not perfection.

Notes

Notes

About The Author

Growing up in a small Tennessee town and getting an education at her state university ill-prepared Mary Boyd Alley for the tremendous challenges she would face in the years to follow.

After working as a medical technologist, she has been a homemaker and pastor's wife for 38 years. Her experiences gained in motherhood, homemaking, personal evangelism, counseling, teaching ladies' groups, and cross-cultural communication have enriched her capacity as a devotional writer. Now she and her husband are involved in world-wide missions.

They live in Central Virginia.

Order Form

Meditations of a Happy Homemaker

To order by phone, please call 800-457-3230
Visa and MasterCard accepted

If you would like to order additional copies of *Meditations of a Happy Homemaker* by mail, please feel free to copy this page and send to:

Winters Publishing
P.O. Box 501
Greensburg, IN 47240

Please send me:

_____ copies at $12.95 each $_____

Shipping: $2.00 1st book,
$1.00 each additional $_____

IN residents include 6% sales tax $_____

TOTAL $_____

Send to:

Name:_____

Address:_____

City:_____ State:_____ Zip:_____

Phone:_____-_____-_____ Email:_____